How To Books

Enhancing
Your
Employability

Enhancing Your Employability

How to make sure you achieve
a fulfilling and rewarding career

RODERIC ASHLEY

How To Books

Cartoons by Mike Flanagan

British Library Cataloguing in Publication Data
A catalogue record for this book is available from the British Library.

© Copyright 1998 Roderic Ashley.

First published by How To Books Ltd, 3 Newtec Place,
Magdalen Road, Oxford, OX4 1RE, United Kingdom.
Tel: (01865) 793806. Fax: (01865) 248780.
email:info@howtobooks.co.uk
www.howtobooks.co.uk

First edition 1998
Reprinted 1999

Note: The material contained in this book is set out in good faith for
general guidance and no liability can be accepted for loss or expense
incurred as a result of relying in particular circumstances on statements
made in this book. The law and regulations may be complex and liable to
change, and readers should check the current position with the relevant
authorities before making personal arrangements.

Cover design by Shireen Nathoo Design
Cover image PhotoDisc
Produced for How To Books by Deer Park Productions.
Typeset by Concept Communications (Design & Print) Ltd, Crayford, Kent.
Printed and bound by Cromwell Press, Trowbridge, Wiltshire.

Contents

List of Illustrations

Preface

WHAT THIS BOOK AIMS TO DO

The world of work is changing fast. This book aims to explore the various factors which have caused the changes in ideas about and attitudes to work, and to encourage you to explore how you can prepare yourself for these changes and gain the most satisfaction from work.

Whatever your work situation – whether you are starting your career, looking for a change of direction, returning to work after a break, facing unemployment or early retirement – this book will help you to understand yourself, your motivations and what you can offer.

In order to gain the greatest value from this book, you, as reader, will need to enter into the 'activities' in a positive frame of mind. You will want to ask yourself some searching and fundamental questions. You may need to discuss various issues with a partner, close friends or colleagues. As well as living with the answers you provide, you can actively seek to enhance those skills and qualities.

Understanding the structure of the book

This book will guide you through that process in stages, so you should aim to read through it in the order printed. Whilst there are sections which you can use as reference sources in the future (eg Chapter 8 Where are you going next?), you will gain the greatest benefit by reading the book in sequence and allowing yourself time to reflect on some of the issues. This book will help you to help yourself by:

- outlining the changing patterns of employment
- explaining the rationale for such changes
- encouraging you to get to know yourself as a worker and a person
- establishing what motivates you
- understanding what you have to offer
- developing your employability skills
- assessing your attitude to life

- establishing where you are going next
- devising your personal action plan.

When you have finished reading this book, you should understand both more about the nature of work today and more about yourself. A number of pointers will have been offered to you but it is ultimately up to you to decide what to do about them. The book does not suggest ideas or ways of life you should follow; it aims simply to open your eyes to these opportunities so that *you* can make *your* decision based upon self-knowledge and understanding.

Take comfort from what you learn are your strengths, have the courage to develop your weaknesses and learn to recognise where you have control over your life and work.

On pages 109 to 112 you will find a list of other sources of support and information. If you are particularly interested in certain aspects (eg motivation theories), you will find a booklist (p 113) to guide you in exploring these issues in greater depth. Special acknowledgement to *Jobshift: How to prosper in a workplace without jobs* by William Bridges (see references). Acknowledgement is also given to the Estate of Robert Frost for permission to include an extract from *The Road Not Taken* (edited by Edward Connery Lathem, published by Jonathan Cape).

If what follows meets those aims, I extend my thanks to family, friends and colleagues for their help and advice. In particular, my gratitude to Moira Ashley for reading drafts of the manuscript, making valuable comments and, more importantly and with my love, for encouraging me to identify and articulate my own employability skills when the solid ground of employment proved illusory.

Rod Ashley

1
Moving from Employment to Employability

UNDERSTANDING HOW CHANGES ARE AFFECTING YOU

This book starts with two premises: firstly, that the traditional job pattern has gone and secondly, that the traditional covenant between employer and employee has also gone – both of them for good. The expectations of our parents for employment (theirs and ours) have disappeared. That does not mean to say that there will be *un*employment, although inevitably there will be some. Rather, it means that whilst there will be fewer jobs, there will still be work. That may appear to be something of a conundrum, so let's start to spell it out.

> **Instead of the traditional employer/employee covenant to which we have all grown accustomed, workers will need to take on a different attitude or 'mind-set' towards the concept of work.**

Rather than the passive expectation of becoming an employee, of devoting x hours a week and y years to a particular employer in return for z salary and a sense of security, there must be a much more active selling of the skills, experience and qualities which each individual can offer.

UNDERSTANDING THE FUTURE OF WORK

The Government's Green Paper published in February 1998 about the future of learning (to equip people with the vital knowledge and skills for a new century) states that:

The information and knowledge-based revolution of the twenty-first century will be built upon . . . investment in the intellect and creativity of people.[1]

Individuals should invest in their own learning to improve their employability, professional competence, and earning potential or for leisure.[2]

The Learning Age

11

Note that the government identifies **employability** as a key issue as we all become knowledge workers in the next century. Indeed, government figures confirm that the last decade has seen fundamental changes to the UK employment scene. There is an increase in the number of part-time workers (now totalling 28 per cent of all workers), of short-term contracts and of people retiring or being retired early. In some cases the percentage of people taking early retirement is staggeringly high. The proportion of people feeling secure about their job has fallen from 96 per cent in 1990 to 43 per cent in 1996[3]. In summary:

- There is a reduction in the level of full-time male employment.
- There is an increase in the level of female employment (not necessarily full-time or permanent).
- There are fundamental changes in working patterns.
- The shift in employment has been away from large employers to small and medium enterprises (SMEs).

Let's take a brief journey through history to examine the changing nature of work from the earliest time to today to see what has brought about these changes affecting us now.

Progressing from stone-age club to gold watch

The Stone Age
Men's task was to provide for their families by meeting their basic survival needs – food, clean water, shelter and warmth. Women's task was to rear children and to cook food brought home by menfolk.

The Iron Age and Bronze Ages
Role of men more sophisticated as they designed and created more intricate weapons with which to slay both animals and human aggressors. Also able to forge small pieces of precious metal – coins – to exchange for other items.

The Middle Ages
Beginnings of international trade and specialisation in work (eg shoemaker able to sell shoes to villages or exchanged for goods/services such as repair to wheel of his cart). Beginning of concept of division of labour and of a service having a cash value.

The Elizabethan Age
Age of Discovery, trade and shops. Concept of division of labour well-established.

Late 18th/19th century
Industrial revolution altered the demographic structure of Britain. Demand for low-cost fuel/reliable water-source brought industry to previously rural communities.

Twentieth century
Introduction of production line concept. Each worker trained to perform a specific task. The production line dependent upon each worker knowing his/her role and contributing to one small part of production process continuously during shift.

WHAT IS A JOB?

All these changes serve to reinforce a key point – that the 'job' is a comparatively recent phenomenon. The first industrial revolution gave almost universal understanding of the concept of a job as

● the social contract into which we enter with an employer to spend an agreed number of hours per week in his/her employment in exchange for a certain sum of money which allows us, within financial constraints, to spend it in the way we wish to pursue a particular lifestyle.

Because we or our parents may always have known a 'job', it is easy to forget that it is not something which has existed from time immemorial and should always continue to exist as part of out social fabric. As we have seen above, until the Middle Ages people certainly had work – but they would have looked at you askance if you suggested that their work would always remain constant throughout their lives and that they would pick up a pension at the end of it.

How were jobs invented
It cannot be over-emphasised that the 'job' is something which emerged with the Industrial Revolution. It was something which in a novel way appeared to offer security, compartmentalising a part of the day into a known group of tasks.

Recent experience of the job has been that, for those in a stable employment situation, the employer would ensure employment until retirement age. Yet for many people, there would be no programmes of retirement planning. One day they would be in full-time work, the next day without work. The final day in work would be marked by a party celebrating the loyalty and achievement of the individual, marking this by the presentation of a gift such as a gold watch to mark the transition from active work to retirement (literally 'withdrawing'). Surely, the symbolism of the gold watch was bizarre – the overtones of value, worth and treasure were also reinforcing the fact that now – perhaps for the first time in the individual's life – time did not matter! There were no fixed schedules or deadlines.

THE DECLINE AND FALL OF THE JOB

In the same way that the first Industrial Revolution of the 18th and 19th centuries had a major impact on people's lives, so too we are undergoing another industrial revolution as we enter the 21st century.

That initial premise of the job was based upon it remaining fixed within a certain and known world. Of course, dependent upon ability, hard work and opportunities, that job might evolve through promotion into a more prestigious and financially rewarding one – but not necessarily a more enjoyable one as we will see in Chapter 4.

What has happened to make job certainty disappear?

The number of people realising that there is no such thing as a permanent, secure job swells daily. The election in the UK of a New Labour government in 1997 brought an upswing in the 'feelgood factor'. Whilst the government has talked of creating more opportunities for employment (and indeed has created some), it has not suggested that full-time permanent employment for everyone will return. Indeed, ministers know that to do so would be unrealistic, insincere and unworkable as it would fly in the face of everything happening not just nationally but globally.

The reasons for such change are varied and complex and have evolved over different timescales. But in summary, there are six principal reasons why this has occurred.

1. The development of a global economy
Consider how many of our consumer goods and indeed how much of our culture is now global. Wherever you go in the world, you will see young people wearing clothes or footwear with names like Adidas, Levi's or Nike. Whether it is in Europe, the Far East or the Americas, the goods will be the same. Adidas, a German company, produces its branded garments wherever the right balance of cost and quality can be obtained. The country of origin is immaterial.

2. Many jobs are at the mercy of changing customer needs
Take one example. Until the 1970s, in any European port a large number

of dockworkers would be required to unload a ship's cargo. Today, most shiploads are containerised, requiring only a small number of highly-skilled crane operators to move the container from ship to dockside storage, to truck or rail-wagon, from the comfort of an insulated cab high in the air. It is not that customers are saying 'We don't want to employ dockers' but rather that they want goods transported securely, safely and with the minimum of handling – with consequent savings in time, paperwork and cost.

3. Technology has changed the nature of many businesses and industries
Substantial technological development allows companies to be more productive with fewer staff. Technology can help drive down costs and drive up consistency of quality. For example, motor manufacturers compare their efficiency on a global scale by quoting the number of labour hours it takes to produce a vehicle.

Take a look in any newspaper or telephone directory for the number of financial services which can be bought 'direct'. From insurance for your home or car to pensions and investments, many companies have established themselves to capitalise on the public's requirement for simplicity of service, longer opening hours and doing away with the customer's need to complete paperwork. In these 'call centres' employees, wearing a telephone headset and sitting in front of a computer screen, transact customer business. This is predicted to become a major form of employment, with many employees being part-time, working flexible or unsocial hours. In some cases, the growth in business crosses borders – a major US insurer uses a call-centre in the Republic of Ireland staffed by people several thousand miles from both headquarters and customers. Likewise, in some cases, the work is not carried out by the insurance company itself but is subcontracted to other companies, which is called **outsourcing**.

4. 'Outsourcing' of work
It is a rapidly expanding phenomenon that many major companies now retain a small core staff for regular operations and buy in additional expertise and labour on a short-term or consultancy basis as and when it is needed. This way the company can reduce its payroll and on-costs, focusing its efforts on its core purpose. When it needs additional staff, it calls on a pool of people to whom it may pay relatively high consultancy rates to deliver specified services 'just in time'. When the contract finishes and the need no longer exists, it no longer has to support these people through the lean times.

For example, in the early 1990s the Ford Motor Company in Britain needed to downsize to retain its competitiveness. This coincided with Ford's need to invest in new engineering as it had contracted to build new engines for international use, as well as enhancing its engineering to meet the demands of recently acquired marques, Jaguar and Aston Martin. Consequently, whilst the company had a programme of redundancy and early retirement for staff over 50, it also created a consultancy base, through which it bought back staff over a short term for their engineering skills as and when needed, but without the long-term commitment to an employee.

5. The contingency worker
Work and hence employment are dependent upon there being a demand for goods, products or services. As we saw earlier, if there is a change in consumer needs but no corresponding adaptation or flexibility from the employer, jobs are at risk. Everyone's work depends upon the organisation achieving results. Of course, the first staff to go in difficult times will be the temporary, part-time staff, but employers the world over are clapping their hands that even well-established, permanent staff can be lost when finances dictate. (Naturally, this can create major problems when economies or companies experience an upturn and don't have the expertise or experience on tap – but that's a separate issue.)

6. A changing mind-set
As organisations become aware of their own fluctuating needs and of how their own long-term strategic planning is limited because of external factors, so they have started to buy in staffing on an 'as and when' basis. This is not unskilled, casual staff brought in by the holiday trade for the peak summer months. The 'new' workforce may:

- be highly intelligent, gifted, creative individuals
- be well-qualified
- have a wide range of experiences and expertise which can be tailored to the specific needs of the organisation buying in such consultancy – whether short-term or long-term.

These are people who know, understand and value their own skills and expertise and can also sell these skills to the appropriate bidder. They put their own personal progression and employability at least on a par with the organisation's objectives.

Changing the world of work
In short, these changes require a fundamentally different outlook on the

world of work. From the static, secure world in the early part of the chapter, we have moved into a world where the essential qualities and skills needed to remain in employment are characterised by William Bridges in his book *Jobshift*[4] as : employability, vendor-mindedness and resiliency. What does Bridges mean by these terms? Let us summarise what he is saying:

- **Employability** is retaining your attractiveness to employers by developing and displaying those abilities and attitudes in demand.

- **Vendor-mindedness** involves starting to think as an external consultant who has been hired to carry out a specific task.

- **Resiliency** is fairly self-explanatory, requiring the individual to be able to find his/her own security from within, by knowing his/her strengths and weaknesses rather than being passively dependent upon some external agency (the traditional employer).

> **Employability is a combination of the changing mind-set and the contingency worker within the global economy.**

RESTRUCTURING THE WORKPLACE

Restructuring organisations has been a major activity of the 1990s, although in recent years the focus has changed. Initially, the purpose was to downsize at all costs – to shed excess capacity, labour, plant and sites in order to achieve a 'leaner, fitter structure'. More recently, the focus has been upon business process, performance improvement, and to involve and integrate employees in this exercise. In particular, the principal reasons cited for restructuring now tend to be: meeting customer needs, strategic planning and team-working.

Flexibility in employment is a key objective – organisations need flexible employees to meet the demands of today's customers for round-the-clock delivery of products and services. This is why some companies have now introduced 'annualised hours' or **job-shares** to give that mutual flexibility.

But flexible employees are also needed to be responsive to changing demands, to take on a wider range of roles and tasks, to switch from project to project at short notice and yet be able to hit the ground running. All this requires competence and confidence in the skills and qualities which may not have been in demand previously.

Handling the issues – the government response

Such major changes as those outlined mean that governments must conduct a radical overhaul of the infrastructure of the tax, social security benefits and contributions systems in order to reflect the flexibility and uncertainty in the labour market. With such challenges in strategic, long-term planning for business, health-care, education and other areas of life, governments must ask questions such as:

● How will people's pensions be paid?

● How can the tax system track the variety of activities in which people may be involved?

● How does the school education system shift from preparing pupils with high levels of static academic knowledge to a flexible working and learning environment in which teachers can no longer sincerely say 'Work hard, get your qualifications and you'll get a good job and a secure career'?

● How does the education system respond to individuals' needs which do not follow the neat pattern of academic years and terms?

Handling the issues – the personal response

For those of us who have been made redundant, 'outplaced', had contracts terminated, reached the end of a fixed-term contract or otherwise been dispensed with, the feelings can initially be complex and difficult. You can feel rejected or marginalised – both personally and professionally; that your professional expertise and experience is not valued; that the organisation's values have diverged widely from your own. You can feel that all the hard work over many years, the loyalty, devotion, goodwill, extra hours and effort, the placing of the job or organisation above your own personal or family concerns, have counted for nought.

You may ask: 'Has the way in which I handled this contract; achieved that target; dealt with that tricky situation; trained those people; implemented this change or become an integral part of the reason that people want to do business with this organisation stood for nothing?' In the words of a former colleague. 'Working for this organisation involves give and take. You give, they take.'

FACING UP TO THE ISSUES

One can sense a range of emotions – not least at the varying degrees of competence with which change management and matters of outplacement have been handled by those who have no concept of the personal feelings of those involved. Indeed, one can question in a professional context the competence of those remaining. 'What valuable skills does X have which I do not possess?' Perhaps X does indeed have specialised skills or a level of competence from which we could all learn. Or perhaps X has been in post so long that it's going to cost too much to make him/her redundant when normal retirement age is just around the corner. Situations like this can be complex, and difficult to analyse and cope with on a personal level, particularly when one is unlikely to have at one's fingertips all the relevant facts upon which corporate decisions have been made.

And, of course, we must remember that for some people the offer of early retirement, voluntary or compulsory redundancy will be eagerly grasped. They have had enough of that organisation, are ready for a change, or for a break from or an end to work. They may take away with them a negative attitude to work and are sufficiently comfortably off not to bother with it again. Good luck to them. Such people are a dying breed, both in terms of attitude and financial well-being – and they are unlikely to be readers of this book. But those for whom a new stage in life beckons and who want to approach work in a more pro-active way than previously, this book is going to help build upon those skills and experiences.

SELF-CHECK QUESTIONS

If you have been in some of the situations described above, it is important to reflect upon and discuss your personal response. You may already have done so – with former colleagues, in the pub or with friends and family. But many people do not discuss the issues of how they feel. Before we proceed, it is important to get such feelings in the open, otherwise they will be at the back of your mind when we are trying to move forward. You can simply jot some points down in the gaps or use the questions as a trigger for a discussion with someone whose opinion and listening skills you value.

If you have been made redundant/outplaced etc, how do you feel about:

- The way in which it was done?
- How it affects your attitude to work?
- How it affects your attitude to life?
- How it affects your opinion of yourself?
- How you feel about future prospects of work?

CASE STUDIES

We will follow the progress of three fictional characters – Jane, Francis and Ramish – as they develop their employability skills. The first set of case studies examines the family influences on their understanding of jobs and work.

Jane starts out on her career

Janes comes from a traditional middle-class British background. Her father was a civil servant who remained with the Department of the Environment all his working life, straight from grammar school. He progressed through the different levels of the Civil Service to a middle management position. His income was sufficient that his wife did not work and she was encouraged to stay at home to raise the family. The family atmosphere was a secure one, based on the dependability of Jane's father staying in that secure and relatively unchallenging environment. Yes, there were pressures periodically, but nothing undermined the notion that her father was an indispensable servant of the people, working in a world somewhat aloof from the perceived 'unpleasantness' of industrial and business life.

Jane consequently grew up in an atmosphere that valued security, avoided risks and expected the State to provide in the future in return for loyalty at work. That embossed crown on her father's briefcase symbolised the dignity and permanence of his employment. Indeed, Jane's friends who were children of the self-employed or those in business were regarded as a little flash.

Jane begins to feel the pressure
Having completed a B.Ed. degree in a respected higher education college, Jane commenced her teaching career well-briefed on the National Curriculum, classroom control and motivating primary school children. But she is not prepared for the mountain of paperwork involved in assessment and reporting, which grows over the years. Recognising that, compared with many other jobs, teaching occupies only 36 weeks of the year, she is also aware that during term-time she puts in a ten-hour day on average.

Francis follows in his father's footsteps

As a child Francis lived in several parts of the country, following his father's employment as a salesman with a major insurance company. Accustomed to the commercial aspect of life, Francis recognised that there could be peaks and troughs in the company's performance.

Fortunately, they were shielded from the troughs and his father went from strength to strength, although his mother would usually have a part-time job just to be sure. There was an expectation that if you fitted in with the company ethos, it would look after you in the bad times, and that future provision was a mixture of company and personal prudence. Francis remembers the long days his father would spend at the office, the sales conferences and the week-long training programmes. 'Work hard', 'abide by the company rules' and 'don't get caught out by using your initiative' were the golden rules his father had instilled in Francis.

Certainly, when Francis finished his compulsory education, he had little inclination to progress to further or higher education. 'I'm just delaying getting a job', thought Francis and he saw how, with his head screwed on the right way, and taking his family's values into the work-place, he could also prosper with his chosen career in the Eastern Bank.

Francis feels adrift

It comes as something of a shock to Francis when his bank is taken over by a larger institution. The cosy world in which he has immersed himself since leaving school disappears overnight, as do several of his older colleagues for whom the prospect of major change is too much. Francis has not realised how steeped he is in company tradition until the clash of cultures with the new company is on him. How will he fit in? Can he adjust? How do other financial institutions operate?

Ramish breaks with tradition

As the son of first-generation immigrants, Ramish was aware of both cultures. Leaving India had been a bold decision for his parents, but based on the promise of a better and more secure lifestyle in Britain and better financial rewards for those who tried hard. Ramish saw this in older relatives who had arrived in Britain a few years earlier – 'Work hard and you will achieve'. Yes, there might be some racial prejudice but there was always work available and Britain seemed to value the ethos of a determination to do well.

Those first few years were tough – a succession of dingy bed-sits whilst the family established itself. Ramish remembers his childhood, living above the corner-shop which had become the family's business. Working 18 hours a day, never taking holidays and the gradual decline of his mother's health were the penalties. But the close community respected the level of service, the chance to buy goods on the slate and the way in which all the family would contribute to the enterprise by delivering shopping, running errands and so on.

From these humble beginnings Ramish saw that there was hardship and suffering among his community and determined that when he grew up, he would help do something to relieve it.

Ramish senses disillusionment setting in
The attraction of working for the National Health Service (NHS) is obvious to Ramish. It offers a quality and breadth of provision he can only marvel at, and the opportunity to contribute to society which he has yearned for since his early days. Qualifying as an osteopath, he starts his career with great enthusiasm and ambition, which serve him well for many years.

However, as he progresses up the career ladder, he also becomes aware of the new managerial ethos, of the purchaser/provider distinction and how the focus is much more upon achieving managerial and business objectives in an environment which has no control over the quality of its raw products, ie patients. Disillusionment and disenchantment are setting in fast.

CHECKLIST SUMMARY

In this chapter we have:

- Outlined reasons for the end of the permanent job.
- Defined the concept of employability.
- Stressed the importance of sharing your thoughts and feelings on these issues.

ACTION POINTS

- Identify someone with whom you can discuss these issues.

2
Getting to Know What You Are

CHARTING PROGRESS

How did you become what you are today? Whatever stage of life you have currently reached, powerful influences have brought you to this stage. These might be educational, sociological or anthropological. They might include influences from family, your peer group, previous employers or other sources. It can be enlightening to reflect on these and to consider how they have influenced us to become *what* we have become.

> **In knowing what we are, we are in a stronger position to determine what we might become.**

Marking milestones

For this next activity, picture two educational experiences you have had – one good and one bad. These experiences can be from any part of formal education at primary, secondary or other education or training. For example, it could be learning maths, learning to drive or learning to crochet. It could be a formal learning situation or an informal one. It really doesn't matter as long as you can identify *one* situation in which you feel you learned a lot and *another* in which you feel you learned little.

For instance, taken from school, an example of the first experience might be: 'We had just started algebra and I found the concepts really difficult. The teacher sat down next to me, gave me some individual tuition, patiently explaining it for several minutes. Then everything clicked.'

Or for the second experience, 'One day the teacher left the classroom for a few minutes and, on returning, found that a lot of pupils were playing around. The whole class was put in detention even though I was getting on quietly with the work set.'

Remember that although these experiences are taken from school, your experiences can be from any aspect of your own education or training.

Recalling experiences

To help you visualise the experience, try to picture the teacher/tutor/trainer in your mind.

Recall experience 1:.....................................

Recall experience 2:.....................................

Having recalled both experiences, try now to assess *why* you have recalled them.

- What is there about these two experiences which sticks in your mind?
- What do they tell you about the way you learn or respond to learning?
- What do they tell you about the way you are motivated or demotivated?

Considering your achievements

Moving on from this, let's now consider some of the real achievements and milestones in your life to date. Frequently, when we think about achievements we tend to think only in terms of educational achievements (x number of GCSE passes, etc). Without devaluing the importance of these, particularly if gained as a mature student in difficult circumstances, they represent only one aspect of our lives. Indeed, the psychologist B F, Skinner said that 'Education is what remains when what has been learned has been forgotten.'

How many other things may we have done where we have felt that there has been no formal recognition of our achievements? Remember that the British educational system traditionally worked by setting up barriers (eg the eleven-plus examination) for most people to fail at in order that only a few could excel. Examples of achievements outside education might include: learning to swim as an adult, acting as a peacemaker between squabbling family members, redecorating the lounge – at last.

IDENTIFYING THOSE WHO HAVE INFLUENCED YOU

From time to time we reflect upon those who have in some way influenced us to make the decisions we have taken in order to become what we are. We know those who have influenced us directly or indirectly, the way they may have inspired us, energised us or encouraged us to take some decision or action. They might be family or close friends. Equally, we may not have known them personally – they might be religious or political figures, authors, management gurus or sports people. The poet

Thom Gunn used the title *My Sad Captains* (from Shakespeare's *Antony and Cleopatra*) to describe those whom he admired and who influenced him during their lifetime.

In this poem, they appear to Gunn almost like ghosts but shining out in the darkness with the brightness and presence of stars. They seem to have the strength of will and perception not to be caught up in the detritus of petty occurrences, but to stand as a beacon of light and influence for those needing guidance and support.

Consider who in *your* life has influenced you, acted as an enabler, opened your eyes or in some way had a lasting impact on the way in which you have evolved. Jot down who those people were and how they may have influenced you in some significant way. If you wish, you can add to the list, but keep it to those who have really had an influence on you.

Those who have influenced you	*How they have influenced you*
. . . .	. . . .
. . . .	. . . .
. . . .	. . . .
. . . .	. . . .
. . . .	. . . .
. . . .	. . . .
. . . .	. . . .
. . . .	. . . .
. . . .	. . . .
. . . .	. . . .

Self-check questions

- Would those who influenced you understand the situation you are in now?
- If so, how would your 'sad captains' be speaking with you now?
- What advice would they give you now that you are considering this change in your life?

IDENTIFYING WHAT YOU DO

Whatever actions have led us to the current situation, much of your life may now be spent carrying out different tasks in particular roles. We each have different aspects to our total being which cumulatively make us the people we are. These different roles might be, for example, colleague, line-manager, trade union official, parent, brother/sister, etc. We sometimes use the expression 'wearing my . . . hat, I think that . . . ' Different roles call for different actions and attitudes and these can sometimes cause conflict. For example, we may sometimes have to discuss with a colleague his or her work performance and perhaps we have to criticise it – poor punctuality, missing an important meeting, ignoring a deadline, etc. It can be hard to do this, yet at the same time it is both expected of us and will certainly cause more trouble if we do not tackle the situation in the early stages before it becomes a real problem.

When that colleague is also a friend, it can be more difficult still. Which hat do we wear – friend, colleague, boss? Do we swop hats at stages during the discussion? If, when wearing a manager's hat, we have had to criticise someone, how do we ensure that when we next see him or her at a social gathering that s/he knows we *are* wearing a different hat? Of course, style of conversation, facial expressions, body language, context can all give the necessary signals. Even so, making the switch between roles – changing the hats – can cause stress.

Filling in the labels with the roles you hold

Identify your own 'hats' or roles. Here are some examples:

- mother
- father
- son
- daughter
- brother
- sister
- relative
- husband
- wife
- partner
- home-maker
- cook
- taxi driver
- counsellor
- mender of broken hearts
- contractor
- customer/client

- colleague
- boss
- manager
- junior
- trade union representative
- team leader
- team member
- opposite number
- mentor
- role model
- coach
- paymaster/mistress
- appraiser
- appraisee
- student
- teacher.

MAINTAINING YOUR EMPLOYABILITY

Being a pest

Predicting the future is an inexact science, to say the least. There can be many factors which bring about or influence changes, as we saw in Chapter 1. A helpful way of trying to assess and understand the likely trends and developments in your own employment sector is to carry out a **PEST analysis**. This may help you get a greater understanding of what is happening and where your organisation thinks it is going. Useful sources of information can be company newsletters, news items in the media about your sector, and internal memos and notices about changes.

A PEST analysis considers in sequence the various factors which may have an impact upon your sector and your own organisation:

- Political
- Economic
- Social
- Technological.

Hence the title. Understanding these can give you a clearer sense of what is happening to the organisation.

Creating a PEST for Francis

Let's see how such an analysis might inform one of our characters, Francis, who works in the financial services sector.

Political changes

These include things such as changes in legislation, requirements to meet European Community standards and the likely impact upon society through a government's desire to bring about a particular change.

What does this mean for Francis? For the financial services sector, recent political factors would include: the election of a Labour government in 1997 (after it had convinced the City that it was business-friendly); the 'naming and shaming' of pensions companies alleged to have mis-sold private pensions; the introduction of Individual Savings Accounts (ISAs) and stake-holder pensions and the decision not to enter the common European currency.

Economic factors

These would include the consequences of implementing an economic policy both nationally and internationally. For the UK this would include the rise in interest rates, the value of the pound sterling and the UK stock market; the consequent rise in mortgage costs, the difficulties for exporters, the drop in the price of imported goods and the value of stock-market linked investments. Consequences of the political decision not to be in the first wave of the common European currency would also be important.

What does this mean for Francis? This might have an impact on the number of mortgages his bank can sell, the competitiveness of its savings products and the nature of the ISAs it launches.

Social trends

This may be directly out of political hands but would reflect the changing mores and culture of the country. To ignore these would be fatal for any organisation.

What does this mean for Francis? This would involve responding to and creating appropriate products and services for: the increasing number of women in employment, flexibility of pension schemes; creating mortgage products which take account of the uncertainty of employment; the desire by people to conduct their financial transactions 'direct' (ironically by phone rather than face to face) during evenings and weekends rather than during a hectic day or rushed lunch-times.

Technological

This is self-explanatory, as we saw in Chapter 1 (for example, the use of call centres and the containerisation of goods in transit). IT skills are important for all workers now at whatever level and those remaining Luddites are doomed to extinction.

What does this mean for Francis? It means getting to grips with IT, ensuring that customer service is as quick, thorough and efficient as possible by using this technology and ensuring that it is not off-putting or worrying to customers who distrust computers. Accessing the Internet to settle a credit card bill or using a phone banking service clearly has implications for staffing levels.

How Francis's PEST looks

- **P**
  Responsiveness to legislation.
  Preparation of and familiarity with new products (eg ISAs).

- **E**
  Products matched to general interest levels.
  Possible new constituency of customers via stakeholder pensions (the financially unsophisticated?).

- **S**

  Changing demography.
  Changing attitude towards women.
  Different working hours?

- **T**

  IT skills.
  Use of Internet to sell products/conduct business.
  Customers' expectations of a rapid, accurate turnaround of documentation.

Creating your own PEST

Having seen how Francis might complete a PEST reflecting changes in his working environment, try devising one for yourself in your working environment:

- P

  ....
  ....

- E

  ....
  ....

- S

  ....
  ....

- T

  ....
  ....

BEING A ROUNDED PERSON

People often feel that all that employers are looking for is someone who can carry out a specific role or function within the organisation – to wear a particular hat. But, as we have just seen, none of us ever wears just one hat. Some people, particularly the self-employed and those with a portfolio career, are changing hats frequently.

Even for those in traditional employment, some jobs require frequent changes. Take a secondary school teacher, for example. Every thirty-five minutes, s/he will change roles to take a different class each comprising individual pupils with individual needs; each time the bell sounds the lesson content will be different, needing to be pitched at different levels; in every lesson the group dynamics and class management skills will be

How confident are you about your current employment?

I feel of value and know that my skills and knowledge are in demand. I can see progression opportunities within the organisation. Should there be organisational changes, I know clearly what I want and am confident of having the right skills to offer. I am confident that I can create and gain fulfilling work within the organisation.   **Positive**

Currently my work and role are valued. I have the necessary skills and aptitudes to perform other organisational roles. My future within this organisation is uncertain and I have no clear sense of either who to talk with or what I should do if my post disappears.   **Unsure**

There is uncertainty about my current post. I worry about the future because I don't think that I have the right contacts, skills or aptitudes to achieve a post I want here. Nevertheless, I recognise that I have plenty to offer and I'm keen to learn.   **Anxious**

My skills are solely job-specific. If this post goes, I don't know what else I could do. I feel very pessimistic about getting another job with this organisation and don't know what they could give me. I have neverbeen encouraged to think about what else I could offer. Is it too late now?

Negative

How confident are you about applying for posts with other organisations?

I am alert to the employment market in my sphere. I an confident that I could gain fulfilling work with another organisation. I am pro-active and constantly seeking ways to develop my employability and to create opportunities for myself.   **Positive**

I have a reasonable understanding of the employment market – enough to know where my strengths and weaknesses are. I don't like the idea of change but am sufficiently realistic to grasp the opportunities offered to me.   **Unsure**

I have always developed job-specific skills but can see now that I need to develop a wider range of skills and qualities. I am concerned that I won't be able to do enough quickly to catch up.   **Anxious**

When I look around the employment scene I feel that I have little to offer someone else. My skills and abilities don't seem to be in demand. I am very worried about not having employability skills.   **Negative**

Fig. 1. Assessing your confidence in your employability.

varied in order to present an accessible yet challenging learning environment. Maybe the teacher teaches several subjects, changing from RE and sociology at A level to Key Stage 3 English. Each pupil will see the teacher differently and will recall experiences of help, advice, encouragement, praise or castigation. Some will have seen him/her on the sports field, in a drama production, or on a Duke of Edinburgh Award weekend, etc. Is it any surprise that teachers can often feel so physically and emotionally drained, maintaining all these separate yet complementary interactions?

And yet, as we have seen with the example above, when a school appoints a teacher, it is not merely seeking a teacher of subject X. It is seeking a team member, someone who will volunteer for out of school activities, someone to bring expertise and understanding of children, ideas, equipment, finance or administration *as well* as subject knowledge. It is all too easy for employees in any field to forget that employers will take the overview of the total contribution to the organisation an individual can bring.

RATING YOUR CONFIDENCE IN YOUR EMPLOYABILITY

Now it is time to turn to the way you respond to the prospect of retaining and developing employability in what you are in your own organisation. How positive or confident do you feel about your employability with your current employer or with another one? Read through the table in Figure 1 and score yourself accordingly.

Interpreting your response
If your personal confidence rating has been low in either case, this book will help you enhance your confidence as your skills improve. If you scored yourself in the top half of the scale, the book will assist you to maintain your employability. Notice that in each case the more positive responses go hand in hand with a pro-active frame of mind – seeking and creating opportunities and taking the initiative. The more negative responses are accompanied by a more passive and reactive role – waiting for others to do something.

CASE STUDIES

Jane considers her place in the team
Jane has now been teaching for some years. She has never felt inclined to seek a promoted post and has consequently not taken on additional

duties voluntarily. Her experience is limited to a single school and to a single job. Of course, being a classroom teacher *does* demand adaptability, flexibility, resourcefulness, initiative and good interpersonal skills. But Jane is also realising that there are other skills she lacks – she is not a very good team worker, preferring to be left to get on with things on her own, and she tends to rely on the head or deputy telling her to do things on a school-wide basis.

Francis reflects upon his PEST

Francis has now worked for two major financial organisations. His qualifications and hard work implementing company policy to the letter served him well under his previous employer. He was aware of all the financial regulations and good practice and dutifully attended job-specific training courses when required. His new employer has a different approach and prizes customer focus, independent thinking (provided it is within the regulations), lateral thinking and initiative. We know that Francis finds this hard. Yet friends in other financial institutions tell him that it's the same anywhere. Francis does not feel confident about rediscovering the old ways with any other employer, let alone landing promotion with his employer. Still, only 19 years, seven months, 23 days to go.

However, Francis has now completed his PEST (see page 27) which has shown him what the likely developments are going to be. He now has to face whether to work with these and keep ahead of the game or to be swamped by the changes.

Ramish recognises his worth

Ramish has always made full use of all staff development opportunities offered to him, whether in work time or his own. As a result he has an impressive range of skills and experiences and has also picked up several professional qualifications. His work within his field has been recognised at a professional level, by being asked to speak at several influential and prestigious conferences, and his professional views are sought by colleagues. All this has been extra work, not freebies. Certainly, it impressed his employers who felt that he was suitable for several forthcoming vacancies. They considered themselves lucky that they appointed him to his current position, as a neighbouring health authority has just come up with a similar post, but on a higher grade. It's probably not worth the extra travelling time and expense for Ramish to consider this one. Lucky that he's just settled into his post now – he would be a great asset to lose.

CHECKLIST SUMMARY

In this chapter we have considered:

- The milestones in your own development.
- The people who have influenced you.
- The roles you have in aspects of your life.
- Your PEST analysis.

ACTION POINTS

From what your PEST tells you about the future of your employment sector:

- What appears positive about this?
- What opportunities might this present for you?
- What appears negative about this?
- What concerns might you have?
- What action do you think you should take to enhance your employability?

3
Getting to Know Who You Are

FEELING COMFORTABLE WITH BEING YOU

So far we have seen some of the major changes affecting the idea of employment and have considered the impact which this has upon people in work. In the last chapter we considered the various factors which have brought you to the position you now occupy as an employee or potential employee (in other words, *what* you are now).

In this chapter we are going to look at some of the factors which have made you the *person* you are today. If we can understand ourselves, we stand a much better chance of finding a working environment which shares those values.

How often when we meet someone do we ask *what* they do? Even where the discussion is not related to our work or workplace, we often don't converse in general. We gradually move the conversation towards 'jobs', not only to find some common ground but also to see where we may be in the employment 'pecking order'. In Western society we can be obsessed with workplace-based notions of comparative status, and perhaps no country has been as obsessed with this concept as Britain! No wonder other nations have found Britain so class-riddled. As such, our conversations can become stilted by focusing too much on 'what' people are rather than 'who' they are as individuals.

It is helpful to understand who you are before you can consider how to gain the most benefit from the opportunities which lie ahead of you.

In order to consider who you are, you need to reflect on your past life.

LIFE-MAPPING

The following activity is a very practical one designed to help you understand how you have reacted to some of the most significant events

34

in your life to date, and how those experiences may affect your response to change now or in the future.

Below is a sample **life-map**, in this case belonging to Ramish (the paramedic in our case studies). Ramish was asked to identify the most significant events in his life, both positive and negative, and to list them. Here is Ramish's list:

1. Enjoyed primary school where I set my sights high.

2. Started secondary school – intimidating atmosphere and made to feel insignificant. Determined to prove teachers wrong.

3. Got good O level results – chose science A levels, intending to read medicine.

4. Grades not good enough to get into medical school. Selected osteopathy at a college.

5. Enjoyed college and socialising.

6. Fell deeply in love with Prakesh, who then rejected me.

7. Got first job and bounced back from disappointment in love by proving competence in work.

8. Death of father. Plunged into grief but eventually emerged with new vigour.

9. Met Mia. Best thing that's ever happened.

10. Promoted into management – frustrated and feeling trapped.

Ramish then plotted these events on a graph, indicating their relative positive or negative rating. His graph is shown in Figure 2.

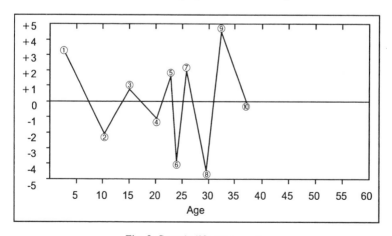

Fig. 2. Sample life-map graph.

Below is a blank life-map. Complete the table in chronological order with your own significant events – you may need to reflect carefully on some of these as some events will come to mind more readily than others.

Making your own life-map

1. . . . .

2. . . . .

3. . . . .

4. . . . .

5. . . . .

6. . . . .

7. . . . .

8. . . . .

9. . . . .

10. . . . .

Now complete the numbered events on the grid in Figure 3, adjusting the age scale to your own circumstances.

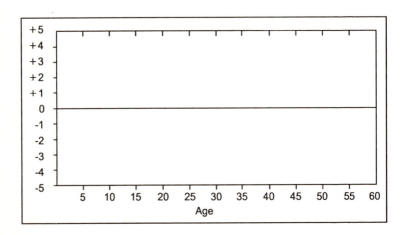

Fig. 3. Plotting your own life-map graph.

What does the chart signify?

If you look at Ramish's list of events, you can see a mixture of positive and negative experiences, the degree of positive or negative rating being apparent from its position in the grid. What is noticeable is that, for Ramish, each negative experience is followed by a positive one. For example, his sense of inferiority at school is accompanied by a determination to do well; his disappointment with his A level results is followed by a successful college course; his rejection in love is countered by the success he found in his work; and the loss of his father enables him to develop new priorities in life. His current situation – frustration in his work and what he gains from it despite his promotion – may be overcome by the closeness of the love and support of Mia who may spur him on to other things.

Your chart may not look like this. Negative experiences may not be mirrored by positive subsequent experiences. However, look at your negatives where they occur. Ask yourself:

- Did the negative episodes provide a learning experience for you?
- If so, what was the positive to emerge from this?
- How did that positive occur – was it just chance or did you make it happen?
- What did the negative experience and your response to it tell you about yourself?

This activity can be helpful in considering how you have responded to previous situations. Have you sought shelter from such painful changes by turning your back on everything outside the safe routine you had become accustomed to? Have you embraced the opportunities which change might offer? Have you learnt how you react as an individual in the face of adversity? Do you feel stronger or weaker in the face of such experiences?

Preparing for the future

Of course, the next step is to prepare for future situations. The next activity is designed to help you project forwards, to enable you to consider how you might want to spend the rest of your life. This is important for assessing your own employability skills because it will help you come to terms with what you want from life, including what you want from work. This activity requires you to think carefully about your dreams, your needs and how you might achieve them. The activity will take you about twenty minutes but you need quiet and to be able to concentrate. You will also need a pen or pencil. If you cannot do so at this stage, put the book aside and plan a time when you can complete the task in one go. Don't skip the activity and read ahead – you'll lose out on a crucial step.

IDENTIFYING YOUR NEEDS AND DESIRES

We often think we know what we 'really, really want'. Few people would turn down a lottery or pools win. Few of us do not dream of holidaying in some exotic location. But for many people these desires are unachievable. The exotic holiday is part of an imaginary lifestyle. The pools win is a catalyst to a lifestyle rather than a desire in itself. At a more mundane level we might desire a more powerful CD player, the latest wide-screen TV or a ride-on motor lawnmower. All of them are 'merely' materialistic *desires* – we can live without them and most of us do.

What we are considering here is what actually drives our innermost *needs*. For many people, these needs can be independent of their financial situation, as long as we are not in poverty. For others, the financial imperative is still there – why do 'fat cats' insist on high bonuses even when they may have phenomenally high salaries anyway? For others, there are more spiritual or literary/artistic drives. Some people need to feel a sense of power or control. Some people are gregarious and always need other humans around them whilst others prefer a more solitary existence. Some people need precise, ordered systems by which to live their lives, whilst others prefer an element of disorder. We are all different and no one way is more 'desirable' than another. (We will look at these human needs in more detail again in Chapter 4.)

LISTING YOUR NEEDS AND DESIRES

To plan the next stages of your life, you need to understand what might be the differences between your desires and your needs. To help you do this, imagine what you will be doing in the future. Often when we do this, we close our eyes. For obvious reasons you cannot do so now! Nevertheless, try to imagine the next stages of your life and to picture a *typical* day over three timescales.

What will you be doing in 12 months' time?

- What will your life be like?
- What will your work be?

● Who will be the important people in your life?

When you have completed your mental picture, ask yourself: How different is 12 months from today? Is it simply projecting your existing life ahead? Maybe you have pictured your children as a year older and at a different phase of their life. Maybe relationships with loved ones have changed. Some of these we might take for granted given the passage of time. But how are *you* different? Have you noted any major or minor shift in you?

What will you be doing in three years' time?

● What will be a good day at work?
● What do you associate with satisfying work?
● What would be a good day outside of work?
● What factors will be absent?

How many of the images you have written down for three years hence are linked with those for 12 months' time? Are there similarities or have you moved on in your thoughts? Perhaps 12 months is too short a timescale to achieve what you really want but there are some glimmers of that achievement over a three-year period. How many of these things have come about by chance and how many because you have been pro-active in making them happen? And if you have been pro-active, when did that process start? What are some of the small, maybe seemingly insignificant things you have done to cause this to happen? Has it been: planning your activities, prioritising demands, saying no to people?

What will you be doing in ten years' time?

● Where will you be living?
● What might a good day consist of?
● What experiences would be pleasurable to you?

Has there been any shift in your images over this period of time? It would be extremely unlikely if there had not. Some of these may be dependent upon your age now. How do you get from now to then? Depending on the life-stage, the time span and your own individual needs and aspirations, you need to decide how you will get there. We will examine how people respond to different forms of motivation in the next chapter.

HOW WILL YOU BE REMEMBERED?

It may seem a rather strange and even unpleasant notion but, if you were to die tomorrow, how might you be remembered? In his famous poem *Afterwards*, Thomas Hardy affects to see the aftermath of his own death, with his idea of what people will say about him. Although Hardy was much more than a nature poet, focusing in his novels on the struggle of humans against a sometimes tyrannical and harsh concept of fate, the lines quoted below give an indication of some of the qualities and characteristics which Hardy felt he possessed:

Afterwards

When the Present has latched its postern behind my tremulous stay,
   And the May month flaps its glad green like wings,
Delicate-filmed as new-spun silk, will the neighbours say,
   'He was a man who used to notice such things'?

If, when hearing that I have been stilled at last, they stand at the door,
   Watching the full-starred heavens that winter sees,
Will this thought rise on those who will meet my face no more,
   'He was one who had an eye for such mysteries'?

Clearly, Hardy sees himself as observant, perceptive and attuned to the natural world with time for animals and nature.

YOUR EPITAPH

Here is your opportunity to confront yourself with how you think people will remember you tomorrow. Don't rush this activity – if *you* can't give the time to do justice to your achievements, who else will? As you consider your own achievements, don't fall into the trap of mere 'conventional' achievements (qualifications or perceived status). Think also of the things which you had wanted to achieve and believe that you have achieved. Again, this will give you an idea of your values, or what you hold dear in life, of the things which you are prepared to give time and effort to in your life.

You can, if you wish, complete the template below to write about yourself.

The death of (name). . . . . (aged). . . . . has just been announced. S/he is remembered principally for endeavouring to. . . . .
. . . .
S/he had always wanted to . . . .

S/he will be remembered for his/her contributions in the sphere of. . . .
. . . .
and will be remembered by . . . .
because of his/her. . . . .

This is how you see yourself at the moment. If you were to write about yourself in 12 months', three years' and ten years' time, how might the memories of you be different? How much would you have achieved of the, as yet, unfulfilled ambitions and needs?

You can, if you wish, develop this into an open epitaph written on the 'headstone' in Figure 4.

Fig. 4. Analyse your needs and desires by writing your 'epitaph'.

Examples can be seen in the case studies below for our three characters, who are beginning to reflect upon their past experiences and to plan their futures.

CASE STUDIES

Jane dips her toe in the water

Jane is doing much the same now as at the end of Chapter 3 but she has become more adventurous in her hobbies and outlook. She has decided to present some of her craftwork at the forthcoming school fete and is hopeful that this will attract orders from parents as well as flag up to the school in a public and visible way her talents in other areas. Jane realises that in her own experience, her reasonable school exam results meant that she was expected both by school and parents to pursue a higher education course and that she chose teaching for negative reasons – she had no strong desire to do anything else. The range of achievable possibilities was not presented to her and, with her civil service family background, it seemed safe to go into teaching.

Francis feels out of his depth

Francis' relatively modest school career meant that he had little prospect at the time of progressing to higher education. The bank seemed a safe and relatively prestigious career. Steady progression up the career ladder was achieved by equally steady, if unstimulating, work and by adhering closely to the bank's procedures. Francis became viewed as a 'company man', well versed in policies and procedures, always checking with the handbook if a problem arose. As a matter of principle, he referred upwards any matters outside the scope of the handbook, thus ensuring that he could not be accused of using his initiative.

On reflection, this has made him inflexible and reactive when the company is taken over and the new culture prizes the ability in junior managers to use a quality which had never been previously encouraged – initiative. That means taking risks and having opinions and, after 15 years, this isn't something Francis takes to easily.

Ramish has doubts about the future

The son of a first-generation immigrant family from the Indian sub-continent, Ramish is rightly proud of his educational and career achievements, despite a few hiccups along the way. Compared with some of his distant relatives, he has done well and enjoys a comfortable lifestyle. He's got where he has through hard work, determination and undoubted ability. His latest promotion into management is applauded by colleagues and family alike but he is not certain that it's taking him in the direction he wants to go. Ramish has had to make hard choices or accept what appeared on the face of it to be a second-best solution previously (college rather than university, being rejected by Prakesh). But he has always seen the positive to come from such situations. He also feels that his career progression at times may have been at the expense of family relationships.

CHECKLIST SUMMARY

In this chapter we have considered:

- The significant events which have shaped your life.
- Distinguishing your needs from your desires.
- How you would like to be remembered (values, principles).
- How your awareness of these issues can shape your future ideas of what you need from work.

ACTION POINTS

- Given the changes you can see beginning to come over Jane, Francis and Ramish, what changes can you feel beginning to come over you?
- How far do you think that you have been in control of your own life or career so far?
- What can you do to take more control of your own life and career from this point? Make a list of the points.

The next chapter looks in more detail at how individuals respond differently to styles of working and analyses which style motivates you.

4
Motivation at Work

WHAT MOTIVATES YOU?

In the last chapter you have had an opportunity to consider some of the factors which have made you the person you have become. You have also considered some of the changes which might come about in the future to help you achieve the sort of lifestyle you seek.

Linked with this is an understanding of the sort of things in the workplace which motivate you – in other words, what makes you tick. Different people are motivated by different things, precisely because we are all different. For example, some people thrive on change and constant new challenges. For others, these constant changes would be very unsettling and, once they have mastered certain tasks performed in a set way, they don't like to see any alteration to this.

In order to understand what it is which motivates people, it can be very illuminating to see what some of the principal organisational psychologists have discovered through their research. We're going to look at some of these findings now.

ELTON MAYO – ACKNOWLEDGING THE HUMAN ELEMENT

Elton Mayo and his team of psychologists conducted some famous experiments in the 1920s and 1930s on 20,000 Western Electric employees at their Hawthorne plant in Chicago. These became known widely as the Hawthorne experiments. A series of tests involving changes in working conditions (hours of work, length and frequency of breaks, lighting conditions, etc) were carried out.

The research team noticed that when adverse changes were explained to staff, when the staff felt involved in the process and felt valued as employees, then any such changes did not reduce production levels. Indeed, production rose to an all-time high and absenteeism reduced by over 80 per cent. Where employees had their conditions changed with no consultation or explanation, and where no one attempted to make the employees feel valued, then production and efficiency both dropped.

What Mayo was *not* saying was that, as long as you are nice to your employees, you can get away with anything. However, he did highlight the importance of the human element – of clarifying with employees the reasons for decisions, of involving them, of taking time to get to know them and explain. In short, by valuing the workforce you are more likely to get more from them, as well as a sense of loyalty, commitment, cohesiveness and self-esteem. Additionally, there will be lower staff turnover and a consequent reduction in staff recruitment and training costs.

Self-check questions
In your experience of work:

● How often have major changes affecting your work been explained to you?

● How have you felt if such changes have not been explained?

● What strategies do you adopt for informing or explaining changes to your colleagues, suppliers, customers, etc?

ABRAHAM MASLOW – SATISFYING IN-BUILT NEEDS

Maslow (1908-1970) argued that all people have what he called a 'hierarchy of needs' – in other words, each group of needs is at a different level. He identified these needs as

● physiological (bodily)
● safety
● social belonging
● esteem
● and self-actualisation, by which he meant realising one's own full potential.

These needs can be represented as in the pyramid in Figure 5.

Maslow's reasoning was that once an individual's psychological needs – warmth, food etc – have been satisfied the individual then becomes more concerned with a safe environment. Once this need has been achieved, the individual progresses to concern with a sense of belonging to a community, such as a partner, a family, a social or religious grouping. Beyond this level of need, Maslow argued, individuals need a sense of esteem, of self-worth. They like to feel valued and to have a role or series of roles, whether these are played out in a relationship, in the community or in the workplace. Right at the peak of the pyramid, Maslow contended, was the need for self-actualisation – and it is only here that an individual's true potential can be realised.

Fig. 5. Maslow's pyramid.

Needs differ according to circumstances

Maslow states that people's needs differ according to their circumstances at any time. For a starving African, the notion of self-actualisation is of no consequence when one's whole being is consumed by desperately craving food. Like any animal, the most important need is to have sufficient food and water for survival. Once this is achieved, the next stage is to seek refuge (perhaps from the rebel dictator's forces who are carrying out 'ethnic cleansing'). Having achieved this level of basic survival, the individual can now focus on the remaining human needs – of social belonging and so on. Thankfully, for most people in our society the bottom two categories in the pyramid are easily satisfied. If we are hungry, we eat and we are merely reminded of the need to do so periodically during the day by slight pangs of hunger. For most of us, satisfying this need is not a problem and we can focus on other needs in our lives, maybe even experiencing real fulfilment. But for the homeless person we pass on the street, a great proportion of the day will inevitably be spent in meeting physiological and safety needs.

However, Maslow's theory reminds us that there are some people who can transcend these needs, despite the circumstances. Gandhi, for example, existed on a poverty diet whilst making his protests about British rule in India, and yet he was able not only to dream of but also to achieve self-actualisation by gaining independence for his nation.

Needs in the workplace
One of the most important tenets of Maslow's view is that, in general, western society is very good at meeting the lower three needs on the hierarchy – physiological, safety and social belonging. What western society is not so good at, he maintains, is giving people esteem and allowing people to self-actualise. This can certainly be true of the workplace.

CLAYTON ALDERFER – LEVELS OF NEED

Alderfer reduced Maslow's hierarchy to three levels, known as 'ERG'.

- *Existence needs*. These include physiological and material desires and equate approximately to Malow's first two levels.

- *Relatedness needs*. These social needs cover the third Maslow level and part of the esteem needs concerned with personal relationships from level four.

- *Growth needs*. These incorporate the remaining needs from level four and the self-actualisation needs.

Self-check questions

- When is the last time you were thanked for completing a task well, or on time or under-budget?

- How much scope do you have with your current employer to develop both professionally and personally?

- How far do you agree with Maslow's classification of needs?

● Can you identify any skills or attributes within yourself which you are keen to bring to fruition in the workplace?

● Can you identify any skills or attributes within yourself which you are keen to bring to fruition in your social life?

DOUGLAS McGREGOR – ALTERNATIVE WAYS OF MANAGING PEOPLE

Influenced by Maslow, McGregor (1906-1964) was particularly interested in the way in which managers treated their workforce and how different management approaches gained different responses. He argued that there are essentially two ways of managing and motivating people, and he termed these Theory X and Theory Y.

Theory X is the authoritarian style. This is based on the assumption by managers that people:

● are lazy
● dislike work
● need a mixture of carrot and stick to perform
● are immature
● need direction and
● are incapable of taking responsibility for their own actions.

This style of management prevailed in the British car industry during the 1970s, for example.

Theory Y assumes the opposite. It is based on the assumption by managers that:

● the average human being likes work and gains satisfaction from it
● in the right conditions, people will voluntarily set themselves targets
● encouragement and reward are more effective than threat and punishment
● people learn not only to accept responsibility for their work but will actively seek it.

Japanese-owned or -influenced car industries reflect this approach with employee involvement through 'quality circles'.

Of course, we must recognise that effective management involves sophisticated and complex tasks requiring a range of approaches and styles to be deployed. Even the most enlightened and ardent advocate of Theory Y recognises that, in order to ensure quality and consistency, you have to be firm and demanding on occasions.

Self-check questions

● Considering your current (or past) employment, in what ways have you experienced a Theory X manager?

● Considering your current (or past) employment, in what ways have you experienced a Theory Y manager?

● In which employment culture do you work better, X or Y?

FREDERICK HERZBERG – IDENTIFYING MOTIVATION AND DEMOTIVATION SOURCES

Working with his research colleagues, Herzberg interviewed over 200 engineers and accountants in the United States in the late 1950s. They discovered that there was a great similarity in the aspects of their work that these employees found motivating or demotivating. These are shown in the chart in Figure 6.

Sources of job satisfaction (*Motivation factors*)	Sources of job dissatisfaction (*Demotivation factors*)
1. Achievement	1. Company policy/administration
2. Recognition	2. Supervision
3. Work itself	3. Salary
4. Responsibility	4. Interpersonal relations
5. Advancement	5. Working conditions

Fig. 6. Herzberg's motivation and demotivation factors.

If we consider the sources of job satisfaction (**motivation factors**), for many people these are the powerful motivators. Even small elements of these factors can make a significant difference to the way they feel about and respond to work. With respect to the sources of job dissatisfaction (**demotivation factors**), these are often areas over which the individual has traditionally had little control, the climate and culture of the organisation dictating the working practices.

For example, Herzberg argued that simply giving a pay rise would not solve the underlying problems. The pay rise would rapidly become the norm and the real problems would remain. This was an issue which both British motor manufacturers and the automotive unions repeatedly failed to recognise during the 1970s, as is shown in the case study below. Herzberg also promoted the ideas of job enlargement, job rotation and of the 'cafeteria' system of benefits. These again were ignored. Real change in attitudes towards work occurs only when workers become involved in taking decisions. The following case study illustrates this.

Recognising values

In the mid-1980s a large building society took over a smaller, regionally-based one. The new culture (**company policy/administration**) was one which had a rigid structure with decision-making being very much 'top-down'. Many of the employees of the former small building society found adjustment to this inflexibility and rigidity difficult. Those who had been allowed a certain element of autonomy and discretion in their work now felt that they were closely-supervised and sensed that they could no longer be trusted (**supervision**). Although the new society paid better than the old one, many employees preferred a slightly lower salary with greater autonomy (**salary**). The larger size and more formal, bureaucratic ethos of the organisation made interpersonal relations more difficult not only between junior staff and middle managers but also between middle managers and senior managers/directors (**interpersonal relations**). Consequently, amongst the former employees of the small society, the environment in which they worked (**working conditions**) was considered to be worse than their previous employment, particularly with regard to the computer system which they felt was significantly worse than the previous one and a source of major frustration.

As a footnote, the organisation concerned obviously needed to rationalise its branch network and workforce, calculating that they needed to lose 200 staff. They were in fact inundated with 1,200 requests for redundancy, indicating that there was widespread discontent and little opportunity for job satisfaction!

Self-check questions

● How does your personal list of motivation factors compare with those identified by Herzberg?

● How does your personal list of demotivation factors compare with those identified by Herzberg?

HOW MOTIVATING EMPLOYEES CAN RESCUE AN INDUSTRY

The British car industry in the 1970s was in serious trouble. The quality of design, production and technology were poor, as was quality control. Working practices in the industry were old-fashioned and strikes were common. The British Leyland company (the forerunner of Rover) had nearly 200 disputes in one year alone. Unions tried to outdo each other in achieving the highest wage settlements.

Getting to the root of the problem

However, the real problem was not money itself. The wages were really regarded as being compensation to the assembly-line workers for the extremely tedious, repetitive and soul-destroying nature of work on the production line. Employees had no say in suggesting improvements or in the overall efficiency of the company. Furthermore, they had no voice to make their concerns known, other than through the unions – which shared management's view of pay levels being the root of all concerns. Jobs were rigidly demarcated. If, for example, as assembly-worker noticed that a conveyor belt needed oiling, he would have to ask a skilled fitter to do it. There was no way that job demarcation rules allowed him to do it himself even if he was able and willing to do so, an oil-can was in reach, or that it would add a little variety and responsibility to his job.

Only when British companies began to adopt Japanese working practices (for example, the collaboration between Rover and Honda on developing new models), did satisfaction levels increase and productivity improve. Such working practices include: active maintenance, quality circles, quality control mechanisms throughout the manufacturing process and establishing a culture of trust, involvement and customer satisfaction through communicating with the workforce.

Creating change

Today, things are very different. Both Rover and Ford have employee development schemes. Both companies believe that workers who are fulfilled mentally and creatively will be more productive and will contribute to the company as fully-rounded individuals. Consequently, each employee is given a £200 allowance to spend on any activity, provided that it is not work-related training (this being catered for separately). Courses as diverse as conversational languages, basket-weaving and learning to parachute have been undertaken.

Of course, there have been a variety of factors other than motivating the workforce which have saved the motor industry. But this illustration proves beyond any doubt that Mayo, Maslow, McGregor and Herzberg were right in their studies and that people do respond to different management styles.

CASE STUDIES

Jane realises the value of consultation

Jane started her teaching career along with the implementation of the National Curriculum. At the time, such a framework for teaching seemed to her and other new teachers to be very desirable. You were told *what* to teach and could then concentrate on *how* you were going to teach it. She couldn't understand why so many of her colleagues were alienated or depressed by it, nor could she believe what she was told about the high number of head-teachers seeking early retirement. As she has gone through her career, and has been part of the 'slimming down' of what became an unwieldy curriculum, she has begun to see how important it is for professionals to be consulted and involved in decisions about the curriculum. Even if Jane now sees her future outside of teaching, she has learnt the crucial nature of professionalism and that consultation with people who feel passionately about what they are trying to achieve in their work is vital to achieve change.

Francis identifies his preferred work ethos

As Francis looks back over his career with the bank, he sees how the management culture of the former owners did not encourage him to develop or express his opinions, to become involved in decision-making or to suggest ideas or improvements. He regarded himself as a good employee, who meekly did as he was told, going by the book and without challenging anything or anyone. No wonder he didn't take to the new owners' style: suggestion boxes, customer clinics, focus groups – all 'trendy talking shops'. But beneath the gizmos, he can see that the new regime actually takes the feelings and aspirations of both employees and customers seriously and that for new, young employees, the bank is a good employer. For those 'rather long in the tooth' with 20 years' experience like himself, it is too painful to change, to admit weaknesses and to develop a sense of ownership of his own aspirations and career.

Ramish rejects the employer's ethos

Ramish has always enjoyed the practical and professional aspects of his work and knows that he is good at them. It's the managerial ethos he cannot come to grips with. He entered the National Health Service believing it was a service with the needs of the patients paramount. But in recent years he has felt that the system has lost sight of this and is playing at being a business with its 'purchasers' and 'providers', its 'client-led ethos' and its new managers who have been brought in from the private sector. He's all for efficiency and effectiveness and would be the first to aim for high professional standards. But he doesn't think that the NHS is a caring organisation any more – it seems to be more about satisfying the needs of chief executives and departmental heads than anything to do with patient care. The workload for everyone has rocketed, and staff at all levels now have little time to talk with patients, to reassure them or allay their fears.

CHECKLIST SUMMARY

In this chapter we have considered:

- Some of the principal workplace motivation theories.
- Your workplace motivation factors.
- The way in which many employers have identified the importance of employee motivation.

ACTION POINTS

Individuals are motivated by different factors. After reading this chapter:

- What factors can you identify as very important to your attitude to work?
- As a summary, what personal ambitions and aspirations do you have for your work?
- How far do you feel these ambitions can be achieved:
  - in your current employment
  - if you change employer
  - if you become self-employed?
- What are the barriers to you realising these aspirations?
- What are you going to do about these barriers?

5
Understanding What You Have to Offer

UNDERSTANDING WHAT EMPLOYERS SEEK

The early chapters of this book have reinforced the idea that the old covenant between employer and employee has broken for good and that *your future lies in your employability*. It is not up to employers to provide that which they can no longer do – the onus is very clearly on the employee, on *you*, to make yourself employable in this fast-changing and increasingly complex world. Many employers have changed this employment covenant with their employees and worked hard with them to make them understand. Others have changed the covenant – but just have not told the employees. Those employees who are unable to make this change will be the casualities not only financially but also in what they can get out of life in general.

By this stage, you should also have a clearer understanding of:

● what makes you what you are (Chapter 2)
● what makes you who you are (Chapter 3)
● and what motivates or demotivates you (Chapter 4).

We are now going to consider firstly the **skills** and, secondly, the **qualities** you have to offer.

DEVELOPING YOUR TRANSFERABLE SKILLS

Let's look in more detail at the sorts of skills which employers consistently say they seek.

Transferable skills are those skills which you can take from job to job, from task to task or from context to context. They can serve you well in life and are skills which you develop throughout life – there is never any stage when anyone becomes an absolutely perfect communicator, for example. You refine and enhance those skills constantly through practice, and by facing new situations and challenges.

In today's working environment, it is essential to be able to use a wide variety of skills and to have the confidence to do so. You need to be able to offer such a range of skills to potential employers or clients, as well as to existing ones, to ensure that you are able to undertake work of the highest quality and which is challenging and personally fulfilling.

Employers are becoming much more specific and demanding in terms of the skills they seek. It is no longer good enough to approach an employer, saying 'I've got three A levels' or 'Here's my degree certificate in Biochemistry'. Whatever the level of employment and the nature of the work, employers need people who can:

- work as part of a team
- communicate effectively in a variety of ways
- be confident problem-solvers
- and are willing to take on a variety of complex tasks.

Increasing need for transferable skills

The concept of transferable skills has become increasingly valued by employers *as well* as the qualifications, training and experience you can offer. Such a concept is still relatively new in many educational sectors – for example in both schools and universities – but it is well-established in further education courses and more vocationally-related higher education courses. For example, medical and nursing students will spend some of their course learning about 'bedside manner', breaking bad news or dealing with grief-stricken relatives; engineering students will focus on the 'professional skills' needed to become competent, communicative engineers; trainee lawyers will study how best to present a case eloquently to make maximum impact from a set of given facts.

IDENTIFYING YOUR TRANSFERABLE SKILLS

Figure 7 gives a comprehensive list of transferable skills. Don't be horrified by the extent of them – anyone who can claim to have all of these skills developed to a high standard deserves a halo. Nevertheless, it can be extremely useful not only to understand what these highly-sought skills might be but also to consider how many of these you have and how you have developed them.

As you read through the list, score yourself on how well-developed these skills are. Note down also the tasks or experiences which have given you these skills. These may be from your working life or from other activities. For example, being secretary of a local charity may have made you good at 'investigating what resources are available'; being a

	Basic level skill	High level skill	Experiences which have developed these skills

Problem-solving

- define and identify the core of a problem
- investigate what resources are available
- enquire and research into the available resources
- analyse data/information
- show independent judgement of data/information
- relate data/information to its wider context
- data appreciation: draw conclusions from complex arrays of data
- organise and synthesise complex and disparate data
- apply knowledge and theories
- show flexibility and versatility in approach
- use observation/perceptive skills
- develop imaginative/creative solutions
- use an approach which is sensitive to needs and consequences
- show resourcefulness
- use deductive reasoning
- use inductive reasoning.

Team work

- listen to others
- be aware of own performance
- observe others' performance and use perceptions
- lead and motivate others
- show assertiveness (set own agenda)
- co-operate with others
- negotiate and persuade
- constructively criticise
- produce new ideas or proposals
- clarify, test or probe others' ideas or proposals
- elaborate on own/others' ideas or proposals
- summarise – bring ideas together
- give encouragement to others
- compromise, mediate, reconcile individuals and/or ideas.

Fig. 7. Rating your transferable skills.

	Basic level skill	High level skill	Experiences which have developed these skills

Managing/organising

- identify what tasks need to be done and the time scales involved
- evaluate each task
- formulate objectives, bearing in mind these evaluations
- plan work to achieve objectives/targets
- carry out work required
- evaluate and review progress and reformulate objectives
- cope and deal with change
- withstand and deal with pressures
- ensure appropriate resources are available
- organise resources available
- show initiative
- manage time effectively
- demonstrate sustained effort
- make quick, appropriate decisions
- show personal motivation
- execute agreed plans.

Communication (verbal and written)

- explain clearly
- deal effectively with conflicting points of view
- develop a logical argument
- present data clearly and effectively
- take account of audience/reader in oral presentation/writing
- show evidence of having assimilated facts
- give appropriate examples
- show enthusiasm and interest
- show critical reasoning
- use appropriate presentation techniques
- compare and contrast effectively
- listen and query where necessary
- discuss ideas, taking alternatives into account
- defend a point of view
- assess own performance.

Fig. 7. Cont/d.

mother may make you show 'flexibility and versatility in approach' or being a trade union representative may have made you able to 'listen to others'. We will return to your responses in the next chapter. For now, let's move from thinking about skills to the personal qualities you have as an individual.

BECOMING A SWOT

To consider the qualities you have to offer, you are going to have to become a **SWOT** – but not in the old school sense. You are going to carry out an activity which every business does about itself in order to identify where it is now and where it is going. By now you should have realised that *you* are a business – what is sometimes called 'me plc' – the most precious and valuable business you will ever be involved in.

However, here, your **SWOT analysis** is a breakdown of the strengths, weaknesses, opportunities and threats of your particular situation as a worker. It is what you have to offer. It is about you personally, whereas the PEST analysis you did in Chapter 3 was about your employment sector. The strengths and weaknesses are internal – your inner qualities; whilst the opportunities and threats are the external factors in which you operate – your working environment. A blank SWOT chart looks like this:

Fig. 8. Blank SWOT chart.

Some people like to call it a **SWOD analysis** (strengths, weaknesses and opportunities for development), but let's stick with the usual term to reinforce the idea of you as your own business. The idea is to honestly and openly appraise your own strengths and weaknesses (SW) and to consider the situation you find yourself in (OT). Positive aspects are on the left-hand side of the page, negative aspects are on the right.

For example, Jane from our case studies has drawn up the SWOT chart about herself shown in Figure 9.

S	W
well-educated	poor IT skills
good interpersonal skills	limited range of experiences
flexible and adaptable	no experience of managing
highly-motivated in areas	adults or finance
over which I have control	little motivation in areas
	over which I have no control

O	T
skills outside workplace	competitors with more
long holidays to develop	experience
alternative work opportunities	local competition
can operate from home	can only currently exhibit
could become supply teacher	during school holidays
whilst establishing business	no alternative finance available

Fig. 9. Sample SWOT chart.

Analysing Jane's situation

Analysing her situation in this way has allowed Jane to see clearly her strengths on which she can capitalise. Her level of education, receptiveness to new ideas, flexibility and adaptability mean that she is likely to be able to adapt to a new working environment. Her interpersonal skills would prove beneficial dealing with customers and suppliers. In particular, she is motivated by having control over her working environment which is likely to be the case in self-employment.

But Jane also recognises her weaknesses – she hates computers and has had as little to do with them as possible (relying on her young pupils for advice!); she realises that being within the same job in the same school with essentially the same staff has limited her range of experiences and challenges; she has little sense of business although she takes great delight in working out how much profit her craft 'business' generates; and she realises that where she has not been fully involved in developments, initiatives or implementing changes in education she has found it hard to motivate herself.

Jane's perceptiveness in reaching these conclusions is not all her own doing. She has talked with and sought the opinions of her best friend Lindsey. Jane trusts Lindsey's judgement and, having started her SWOT, Jane talked it through with Lindsey. Until this discussion Jane had not realised just how good she was in dealing with people until Lindsey reminded her of several situations at college which Jane had managed to resolve. Fellow students had looked up to her for this which Jane had not known. Likewise, although Jane felt she was good at managing and motivating a large class of primary school pupils, Lindsey had to remind her that she had never 'managed' in the traditional sense – she had never had responsibility for finances, equipment, or other areas vital to the running of any business.

As for the opportunities and threats, Jane had also discussed her SWOT with her teacher colleague Ceri, who understood the school culture in which they worked rather more fully than Lindsey who was a social worker. Ceri focused on the opportunities for Jane to develop her hobby more professionally during the holidays, and also pointed out a teacher who had taken early retirement from a neighbouring school and who was doing well, albeit in a slightly different craft field. This was unknown to Jane, but was both an encouragement and a competitive threat.

Reflecting on Jane's SWOT

With her list of positives (strengths and opportunities) and negatives (weaknesses and threats), the first task for Jane to consider is:

- Is this an accurate reflection of her position?
- Is she sufficiently motivated by the positives listed to move forward?
- Is she sufficiently determined to address the negatives?
- If so, how can she turn the negatives into positives?

DEVISING YOUR OWN SWOT

Having seen how the process of devising a SWOT analysis works, now is the opportunity for you to devise your own. Think about the issues discussed in the previous chapters and your own response to these. Think about how Jane (who is perhaps a very different personality in a very different position) has gone about creating her SWOT. To help you:

- Be prepared to take some time to devise your SWOT and to revise it in the light of reflection and discussion. The whole process might take you some days – even weeks.

- Identify someone/several people with whom you can discuss your SWOT. Choose people close to you whose opinion you value and who will give you an honest appraisal. This is not the time for false praise.

● Don't underestimate the power and value of this critical support.

● Think about as many aspects of your life as possible (the 'hats' you wore in Chapter 2) to arrive at a rounded view of yourself.

● Assess whether you have the willpower to deal with the negatives as well as taking credit for the positives.

● Identify how you can turn your negatives into positives.

Here is your blank SWOT chart to complete.

S	W
O	T

Fig. 10. Complete your own SWOT chart.

DESCRIBING YOURSELF

In carrying out the SWOT analysis you have had to think about the sort of person you are. You have had to describe yourself. That is something which many people find difficult to do because they are not used to being self-critical. Take the opportunity now to describe yourself, *in three words only*, as:

● an employee
● a colleague
● a partner
● a family member
● a human being.

Take as long as you need for the activity but don't agonise over choices – a gut reaction may be more accurate. Fill in your responses next to each category.

Below is a list of adjectives. Compare this list with what you have written above.

● Is there anything which you would add to your lists?
● Is there anything you would amend?
● Where there are 'different sides of the same coin' (for example, a 'perfectionist' and 'pedantic'), which is the more accurate for you?

As with the SWOT chart, you may find your list useful to talk through with somebody you trust.

creative	adventurous	numerate
sensitive	thorough	cautious
organised	eccentric	able to plan long-term
prudent	aggressive	a bully
dynamic	extrovert	can see potential in people
assertive	gregarious	fair
patient	methodical	good negotiator
flighty	compassionate	able to take an overview
persuasive	unpredictable	good interpersonal skills
generous	polite	self-aware
punctual	profligate	persistent
competitive	nit-picking	pedantic
quick-thinking	charismatic	financially astute
ambitious	loyal	prepared to take a gamble
timid	ruthless	unbiased
inconsistent	leader	sexist
single-minded	enthusiastic	able to plan short-term
cynical	reliable	egotistical
determined	flexible	authoritative
perfectionist	trustworthy	overbearing
dependable	good time-manager	able to delegate

Having examined all the possible words here (and any others you would add yourself), reduce this list to three words in total. These are the three words which, in any situation, you feel summarise your character most accurately. These are the words you can live with if there were to appear on a badge you wore. Transcribe these words on to your badge and keep these in your mind as you go through the activities in the rest of this book.

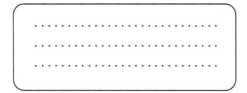

Fig. 11. Your self-description badge.

CASE STUDIES

Each of our characters has now carried out a SWOT analysis like the one Jane did on page 59. In order to move forward with their lives, they have to decide what, if anything, they will do about their weaknesses.

Jane become pro-active

Jane decides to:

1. Become more pro-active in her use of IT. Rather than relying on pupils to guide her, she has enrolled, at no personal expense, on an in-service computer training course.

2. Enrol at her local FE college for a part-time evening basic business management course designed specifically for those thinking of becoming self-employed.

3. Set herself the target of renting a stall at a craft fair in a neighbouring town during the next half-term holiday to sell her wares. Jane has two months of weekends and some evenings to create sufficient stock – a reasonable deadline which won't interfere with her school commitments.

Francis bites the bullet

Francis finds the SWOT analysis difficult to complete because he has not been used to thinking in a self-critical and evaluative way. Nevertheless he has:

1. Taken the courageous step of enrolling on a weekend assertiveness-training course at the local residential adult education centre. He has received full encouragement from his wife to do this.

2. Volunteered to become a departmental representative on a working

party in his bank. This, he hopes, will develop his communication and interpersonal skills as well as showing that he has a lot of experience to contribute to the company.

Ramish devises a plan

Over the last few months Ramish and his partner Mia have spoken about the future on many occasions. They find the structure and discipline of the SWOT analysis helpful and enlightening. Although Ramish has thought and read extensively about a possible career change, he has now:

1. Decided to attend a weekend conference on complementary medicine within the National Health Service.

2. Used his professional expertise and thirst for knowledge to approach a health service journal about writing an article on 'The clinical effectiveness of complementary approaches to osteo-arthritis'. Which-ever way his career takes him, Ramish feels that acceptance of this article in a prestigious journal can only do him good.

3. Volunteered his services to his local GP surgery as a member of the patients' panel.

In each case, our characters have identified ways in which they can move forward both personally and professionally. Notice also how they have made full use of the opportunities afforded to them by their existing employers or current employment sector. They are showing the additional skills and qualities which they have to offer their current employer, which is no bad thing if they should decide to stay where they are.

CHECKLIST SUMMARY

In this chapter we have considered:

*   The importance of developing your transferable skills.
*   How to identify your current transferable skills.
*   Devising your own SWOT analysis.
*   Describing your own personality.

ACTION POINTS

*   Keep your own SWOT analysis up to date.
*   Seek opportunities to enhance your transferable and other skills.
*   Learn to read the developments and needs in your own organisation as well as identifying how your skills and experience can transfer to other organisations.

6
Developing Your Skills

OFFERING MORE THAN QUALIFICATIONS AND EXPERIENCE

The world in which we live involves us carrying out a range of different roles simultaneously, as you saw in Chapter 2. People may be involved, to varying degree, in a variety of different tasks in which they have a specific role. The role may be different in each case, depending on the number of people involved – ranging from solo work to being part of a large team. However, maintaining this range of activities – this portfolio of employment – requires a clear understanding of one's own role as well as that of others, in addition to the ethos of the organisation/s one is working with. In such a world, the way in which people interact with each other also changes.

Structuring through hierarchy

The traditional working environment has usually been as reflected in the **hierarchical organisation chart** in Figure 12.

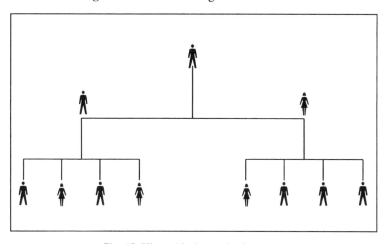

Fig. 12. Hierarchical organisation chart.

Your relative status is indicated by how far up the chart you are. Whilst the vertical channels of communication and responsibility are clear, the chart is static and inflexible. There are apparently no systems of horizontal communication with immediate colleagues or those in different disciplines (eg between marketing and production).

Structuring through teams

An alternative and increasingly common structure is that for **clusters of teams** within an organisation, as shown in Figure 13.

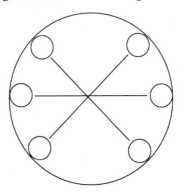

Fig. 13. Inter-team organisation.

Here the individual teams have clear means of communication with fellow team members, and also down the spokes to a central coordinating body which ensures effective 'inter-cell' communication.

Structuing through consultants

For the **freelance consultant** at the hub of the wheel in Figure 14, the structure will be different again.

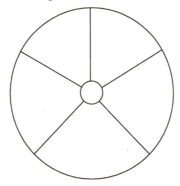

Fig. 14. Consultant-based organisation.

The consultant makes contact down the spokes of the wheel, with all his or her clients around the rim. To the clients the consultant is not at the hub of *their* wheel, but as outlined in Chapter 1 such consultants are brought in to perform specific tasks 'just in time' and are crucial at that stage. Inevitably some distance is always maintained between the hub and the rim, otherwise the structure collapses. Such a way of working is increasingly common and some experts[1] predict that, by the year 2020, 20 per cent of people will be self-employed.

What is evident from any of these illustrations is just how important effective and clear communication skills and team-working skills are in today's working environment.

COMMUNICATING EFFECTIVELY

We communicate principally through the four means as in the chart in Figure 15.

	Learned	**Used**	**Taught**
Listening	First	45%	Least
Speaking	Second	30%	Next least
Reading	Third	16%	Next most
Writing	Last	9%	Most

Fig. 15. The four ways of communicating.

What strikes you as odd about this chart? The skill areas in which there is greatest teaching are in those forms of communication we use least (on average, in Western society). There will be exceptions – for example, people whose work depends upon frequent and sustained written communication. It also true to say that the written communication of, say, a job application form or letter of application are perhaps some of the most important communications we make. But in ordinary social interactions, the degree to which we use a particular means of communication is in inverse proportion to its apparent importance of being taught!

As you can see, we are very rarely taught to listen yet we spend more of our time listening to other people than we do in any other form of communication. Perhaps because we can hear in the womb it is assumed that we know how to listen. Is it any surprise that we can often get things wrong? How often have you heard people say of others, 'He's a poor listener' or 'She never hears what I say'? Of course, we never say it about ourselves!

To illustrate the point, let's carry out an activity. You'll need someone to help you with this, so if it is not convenient at the moment, come back to the activity and don't look at the boxed section below.

Listening actively

Activity instructions
Ask someone to read out the following information to you. Listen carefully and make a note of anything you need to. You will be asked a question at the end.

> You are the captain of a cross-channel ferry. On the first voyage of the day from Dover to Calais you have on board: 29 cars, four trucks, two coaches, ten foot passengers and a total of 132 passengers
> On the first return voyage you have on board: 37 cars, eight trucks, four coaches, 36 foot passengers and a total of 274 passengers.
> How old is the captain?

The answer you should come up with is obvious. But how often do we miss the first piece of information given to us – yes, you should have got it by now!

HOW GOOD ARE YOU AT TEAM-WORKING?

At work you will often work with groups of others. Sometimes you might work with a team. What is the difference between a group and a team? Try to write a definition of a team below.

A team is: . . . .

. . . .

. . . .

We all know what a team is in a sporting sense – a band of people with the same aims and goals, with complementary strengths and skills. The same is true of the workplace. Just as you don't expect in a sports team that all team members can excel in one particular aspect (eg all of them to be fast, light players on the wing, able to outrun their opponents rather than having a more supporting role, literally adding weight to the team), so different skills are necessary in the workplace.

Defining a team

A team has:

- a clear purpose
- clear, shared aims
- clear sense of individual roles
- strong leadership.

TEAM-WORKING WITH COLLEAGUES

Take a moment to reflect on your work over the last week.

- Think of the people you have worked with.
- Think of your role/s and of their roles.

Now consider: In my dealings with all these people over the last week, to what extent have I been working as part of a group and to what extent have I been working in a team?

List the group events:

-
-
-

List the team events:

-
-
-

How good do you think you are at being a team player?

Below are some of the key characteristics of team-working:

- able to take instructions
- aware of own role
- aware of team's aims
- aware of team's purpose
- able to support team members
- able to contribute fully to the work of the team

and of the leader:

- able to lead a team
- able to gain the trust, support and respect of team members
- able to make decisions
- able to delegate authority.

The management writer R Meredith Belbin, in his famous book *Management Teams – Why They Succeed or Fail*, determined from his research that there were certain key qualities in effective teams. It makes fascinating reading, but essentially he noted that successful teams contain:

- A **co-ordinator**: chairs effectively, is able to get the most from team-members, orchestrates the actions of others.

- A **doer**: a reliable person who sees actions through, can be prone to perfectionism.

- A **thinker**: a strategist – maybe better at thinking of applications and implications than actually doing.

- A **supporter**: reliable, can always be counted on to be there and do things, likes to create a co-operative atmosphere.

- A **challenger**: gets the team thinking about what it's doing, perhaps rather prickly and not easily satisfied.

Belbin uses different terminology from the above simplification, but what he stresses is that a team should comprise a number of different personality traits, as above. If all the team members have the same traits, or if these different roles are not included in the team, the team will fail to meet its objectives. So whilst you don't need to be of a certain personality type to be an effective team member, being able to work as *part* of a team is crucial, even if you are not the captain.

SEIZING OPPORTUNITIES TO ENHANCE YOUR SKILLS

Whatever line of work you are in, there will be opportunities to enhance your employability skills. Remember that these are skills which have a value to your current employment as well as to yourself, so seeking to enhance them will also benefit your current employer. You don't necessarily have to look too far – remember that in many aspects of our working life there are positive opportunities and challenges masquerading as insurmountable problems!

Opportunities you can seize:

Opportunity	Gain
Attending meetings	Discussion/debating/chairing skills
Making a presentation to colleagues/clients/suppliers	Verbal skills
Taking minutes of meetings	Writing skills
Writing reports	Writing skills
IT skills	Computer literacy/expertise
Organising an event	Organisation/budgeting skills
Team membership	Teamwork skills
Team management	Management/leadership skills
Training a colleague	Training/mentoring skills

The above is only a short list of possibilities. There will certainly be others which you can identify in the gaps.

CONTRIBUTING TO MEETINGS

Let's consider how you might develop your skills in just one field – for example, contributing to meetings. Most people will attend meetings in some capacity or other, whether in the workplace, as the occasional part of a club or society or some other social gathering, eg church or synagogue. Here is a list of some of the points you might ask yourself about your contributions to meetings:

Making your contributions to meetings

	Yes	No
Do I listen carefully to the contributions of others?		
Do I speak up when I have something to say?		
Can other people hear my voice?		
Do I make eye contact with people?		
Do I leave a meeting wishing I had made a point?		
Do I feel that I have explained the point/s clearly?		
Do I help to create a constructive atmosphere?		
Do I offer support to others?		
Do I talk too much?		
Do others' eyes roll when I start to speak?		
Do I use appropriate body language to reinforce my point?		
Do I find myself lost for words or tongue-tied?		
Do others comment on my performance?		

Do I feel myself blushing?
Do I feel confident about making contributions?
Am I easily influenced or swayed by others?

Chairing meetings

Yes   *No*

Do I ensure that the right people are there?
Do I keep to the agenda?
Do I have a clear agenda and purpose?
Do I indicate the likely finishing time?
Do I create an atmosphere where people can participate?
Do I encourage people to participate?
Do I keep fair but firm control of proceedings?
Do I listen carefully to others?
Do I make 'listening noises' to show that I'm listening?
Do I periodically summarise so that everyone understands?
Do I ensure that decisions are reached fairly?
Do I ensure that decisions are recorded clearly?
Do I ensure that anyone absent is informed of decisions?
If I have a meetings secretary, do I ensure that s/he
  understands her/his role?

You can also devise similar checklists for other tasks and activities in which you might be regularly involved.

CASE STUDIES

Jane recognises her potential

Jane has now attended both of her in-service training courses on using computers and some of her college courses on running a business. She no longer feels over-awed by computers and this has given her self-confidence a tremendous lift. She feels excited about the prospect of running a business and feels that she is temperamentally suited to many aspects of the work.

Several of her colleagues comment on her new enthusiasm and even the head has noted the spring in her step. Jane knows that there are still many obstacles to overcome and her natural caution is proving an asset here. At least she knows that she doesn't have to make a decision in a hurry.

Francis has taken the plunge

Likewise, Francis attends his assertiveness-training course. He dreads it as the time approaches and longs for a heavy cold or something to prevent him attending. But his wife will have none of it and packs him off, delivering him to the door. Francis finds it emotionally draining with role-plays and self-evaluation, but also uplifting and fulfilling. He feels he learns more in that weekend than in all his previous courses at work. It is money well spent. Indeed, his wife cannot believe how exhilarated he is.

The first meeting of his working-party goes superbly and he is impressed with the way in which he presents his views confidently and fluently. He overhears several colleagues say 'Never knew he had it in him'. His growing self-confidence means that he has a new attitude to his work and is ready to consider all future possibilities in a positive light.

Ramish makes progress

Delighted to have had his suggestion for an article accepted, Ramish has thrown himself into completing writing it. He has also now had several meetings of the GP surgery's patients panel and has been pleasantly surprised at the ground-swell of support he has detected for complementary medicine. As this is not initiated by him, he feels that there is genuine support for such provision. One of the GPs appears particularly well disposed towards the concept and Ramish has had several further discussions with her. Nothing concrete yet, but at least it's encouraging.

In the meantime, Ramish has a new lease of life for his job but is perceiving it now in a different way, focusing on what can be achieved through complementary medicine rather than alternative medicine. The different is subtle but Ramish senses that his traditional medical colleagues are now more prepared to discuss issues with him rather than regarding him as slightly odd. The weekend conference on complementary medicine he attends provides some stimulating discussion and useful contacts. He has learnt recently that the UK now has its first Professor of Complementary Medicine (at the University of Exeter, School of Post-Graduate Medicine). His partner Mia is delighted with the progress made by Ramish both professionally and personally.

CHECKLIST SUMMARY

In this chapter we have considered:

● The importance of communication skills.

- The importance of teamwork skills.
- Ways you can enhance your skills.

ACTION POINTS

- Identify skills which you need to enhance.
- Identify specific ways in which you can enhance these in your current employment.
- Identify ways in which you can enhance them outside of work (eg by taking on a role in a club to which you belong).

7
Assessing Your Attitude to Life

RECOGNISING YOURSELF

By now you should be gaining a much clearer idea of your own values and aspirations. Don't worry if they are not yet all crystal clear – such a process takes time and only by reflecting upon your experiences, strengths, areas for development, worries and concerns are you able to move forward into identifying what is right for you. Remember that you are making a decision about 'me plc' and you will never make more important decisions.

Let us start this chapter by briefly summarising where you have reached so far. You have considered:

- what has made you what you are
- what has made you who you are
- your life-map
- your needs and desires
- your SWOT analysis
- your PEST analysis
- your areas for development in terms of skills.

As Cardinal Newman is alleged to have observed, 'The only evidence of life is growth' and you are now on that journey of personal growth by starting to recognise and respond to the issues above. Let's continue that journey.

IDENTIFYING YOUR PERSONAL VALUES

Below are some statements about your attitude to life for you to consider. There are no 'correct' answers but there should be a pattern which emerges with what is appropriate to you.

Recognising what is important to you in life

From the following values, tick the ten most important ones for you.

- personal integrity ☐
- exerting power and influence ☐
- personal space/time to myself ☐
- being competitive ☐
- family/loved ones ☐
- physical and mental health ☐
- spiritual fulfilment ☐
- creativity ☐
- holidays ☐
- a sense of helping/providing a service to others ☐
- personal sense of success ☐
- winning ☐
- fulfilling work ☐
- close friends. ☐

From the ten which you have selected, draw cartoons of the five most crucial ones to you. You don't have to be an artist – just use your imagination to depict the ones of most importance to you. For example, if you include holidays you might draw your favourite resort, if it is physical and mental health you might draw someone running, etc.

Knowing how you would like to spend your time in work

From the elements of work listed below, select those ten which you most enjoy (or with some justification think that you would enjoy).

- providing strategic/corporate leadership ☐
- influencing change ☐
- increasing efficiency and cost-effectiveness ☐
- strategic planning ☐
- 'hands-on' involvement ☐
- analysing numbers/accounting ☐
- meeting deadlines ☐
- being creative/innovative ☐
- negotiating with clients/suppliers ☐
- project management ☐
- developing people ☐
- facilitating teams ☐
- 'making a difference' ☐
- managing change ☐

- problem-solving.   ☐

Again, picture yourself in this type of work. If it is analysing num-
bers, you might show a calculator, if it is problem-solving you might
draw a big question mark then put a line through it, etc.

Choosing how you would like the working atmosphere to be

Having identified the sphere or nature of work which you find most
attractive, how do you foresee the favoured working conditions?
Irrespective of whether your favoured employment is with a huge multi-
national conglomerate, a small or medium sized enterprise (SME) or a
one-person band, what sort of working environment do you favour? This
does not mean, for example, a non-smoking environment, but the overall working relationships and atmosphere. Put a tick in the appropriate
spaces below.

- enough time to do what I need to   ☐
- no unnecessary stress   ☐
- meeting challenges   ☐
- feeling able to decline extra work   ☐
- not over-working   ☐
- regular feedback from my line-manager   ☐
- clear lines of communication   ☐
- good relationships with my superiors   ☐
- good relationships with my peers   ☐
- good relationships with my subordinates   ☐
- support for my endeavours   ☐
- feeling valued   ☐
- a sense of excitement and flowing adrenalin ☐
- corporate goals/mission clearly understood   ☐
- able to delegate appropriately to others.   ☐

Again, draw a representation of the five characteristics you would
most value. For example, if it is clear lines of communication, simply
draw some arrowed lines; if it is good relationships with peers, draw
three smiling faces on the same level.

WHAT IS YOUR ATTITUDE TO LIFE?

How do your friends describe you? As a realist, an optimist, a pessimist
or cynic? They may not necessarily know the 'real' you but others'
views can be accurate. More importantly, if your proposed future life

involves an element of risk, you need to be of a particular disposition. If your anticipated future career is as a self-employed underwater tap-dancer, you would need certain qualities and attributes: the ability to swim and dive, to look aesthetic in your actions, to have powerful lungs and all-round fitness. But on top of this you would need to be an optimist that your endeavours would succeed in attracting a sufficiently large audience and to be a risk-taker, not only physically but also financially. If you are temperamentally ultra-cautious, then no matter what your ambition is, you should forget the project. It just wouldn't work for you. Clearly, the example is absurd, but sometimes we may be blind to certain characteristics which we have and ignore the way in which others can see them.

Establishing your own outlook on life is vital in thinking about which direction to take for the future. Let's carry out a few activities to demonstrate this.

Activity 1

Look at the well-known proverbs below and indicate whether you agree or disagree with them:

1. You can't have the penny and the bun.   *Yes*   *No*
2. What you gain on the swings, you lose on the   *Yes*   *No*
   roundabouts.
3. God helps those who help themselves.   *Yes*   *No*
4. All's well that ends well.   *Yes*   *No*
5. Don't count your chickens before they're hatched.   *Yes*   *No*
6. You learn something new every day.   *Yes*   *No*

Activity 2

Take a look at the pairs of well known proverbs and phrases below. Tick the one which is more in tune with your philosophy or outlook on life.

1. You're never too old to learn.
2. You can't teach an old dog new tricks.
3. No smoke without fire.
4. Every cloud has a silver lining.
5. If something can go wrong it will.
6. It'll be alright on the night.
7. Many hands make light work.
8. Too many cooks spoil the broth.
9. Look before you leap.
10. Nothing ventured, nothing gained.

Activity 3

Look at the picture below. What do you see?

Assessing your answers

What were your responses to these activities?

Activity 1: Proverbs 3, 4, and 6 are optimistic; 1, 2, and 5 are pessimistic.

Activity 2: Proverbs 1, 4, 6, 7 and 10 are optimistic; 2, 3, 5, 8 and 9 are pessimistic.

Activity 3: To you, was the bottle half full or half empty?

If you erred towards the more pessimistic interpretations of the above, then maybe you are by nature a pessimist or cynic. If you erred towards the optimistic, then that is likely to be your disposition.

ARE YOU AN OPTIMIST OR PESSIMIST?

An optimistic person is usually able to deal with disappointment more easily and to bounce back from the trials of life, whereas the pessimist may give up rather too easily and imagine difficulties where there aren't any. Of course, there can be a danger in being falsely optimistic, of not seeing the dangers, problems or difficulties which may lie ahead (just like the underwater tap-dancer earlier). It is often said that the difference between Shakespeare's comedies and his tragedies is not so much in the plot but rather in the disposition of the characters to deal with the adversity they face. In the comedies, the main characters have sufficient strength of character to turn potential misfortune to their advantage, whereas in the tragedies they become overwhelmed by the situations

	Factors present in current work	Factors I wish to retain	Factors I wish to reject
Regular income			
Opportunity to enhance basic income			
Paid holidays			
Sick pay			
Company car			
Sense of fulfilment			
Externally-imposed deadlines			
Self-imposed deadlines			
Pension			
Welfare scheme			
Training/development			
Autonomy			
Work at home			
Nights away from home			
Travel (at my discretion)			
Travel (on someone else's instructions)			
Valued colleagues			
Externally-imposed discipline			
Self-imposed discipline			
Intellectual/mental stimulation			
Boredom			
Challenge			
Insurmountable difficulties			
Negative stress			
Positive stress			
Infrastructure (secretarial/IT support, etc)			
Job satisfaction			
Creativity			
Sense of identity in organisation			
Sense of self-identity			
Set routine			
Variety			
Clear guidelines			
Red tape			

Fig. 16. Assessing what's important to you.

with which they are faced, which become insuperable through the tragic flaw in the character's personality.

Such a difference in mind-set is important, particularly for those considering embarking on a change of career or job, or going into self-employment. You have to consider the likely changes which will go with that shift in work, to ask what you value in your current job or role which may not be there in other jobs.

KNOWING WHAT SUITS YOU

Figure 16 gives a list of the factors which you may have to consider. You will notice that the term 'security' is missing from the list – it may be more apparent in some work than others but, as this book has shown, it can be illusory. There is no one set of desirable responses here – rather, it is a question of the working style and ethos which best suits your personality. However, you should ask yourself some basic questions.

Assessing what suits you

● If a set routine, a known and regular income and being able to take for granted all the infrastructure of a large organisation is important to you, would you be able to work for a small organisation where a variety of roles are expected, or work for yourself?

● If your list comprises mostly negative factors, where will a more positive working environment be found?

● If your current work offers a mixture of positive and negative factors, can you identify which ones you could take with you and which ones you would be happy to leave behind?

Psychometric testing

An extension of such reflection is **psychometric testing**. This involves interpreting your response to a battery of multiple-choice questions relating to your work and social outlook. It is based on the premise that people are suited to different occupations and occupational sectors according to their psychological make-up. Furthermore, that given certain responses, some people should avoid specific occupations! Some companies use psychometric testing as part of their recruitment process, particularly if the job involves selling to the public. A number of psychological counselling centres offer this valuable service. The process will cost you quite a lot and may take half a day. You have been going through a similar process whilst reading this book, but obviously without direct feedback from a psychologist.

CHECKING THE LIFEBOAT

By now you are beginning to get a feel for what best suits you. You need to take into account a number of factors:

- your temperament
- your aspirations
- your skills
- your experience
- your qualities and
- your individual situation.

However, as you have seen, life is not always neat and tidy and things don't always fit into place – and that is certainly true today of careers. How many times have you taken a decision in life which has proved to be beneficial – or otherwise? Think back to the life-map you drew in Chapter 3. How many of those major influencing events in your life were subsequently revealed to have been major turning points because of decisions made?

There are times when you have to make uncomfortable decisions about your working life and employment, yet at the same time be comfortable with living with the consequences of those same decisions.

If you stay where you are

- There may still be uncomfortable times ahead.
- Things may not get better.
- At least it is a known environment and situation.
- 'Better the devil you know than the one you don't.'

If you jump

- Do you know where you are heading?
- Is it out of the frying pan, into the fire?
- Is it a leap in the dark?
- Or is it a question of jumping ship before it goes down?
- Or of jumping before you are pushed?
- Can you accept an element of risk?
- What element of risk can you accept?
- Can you live with the consequences of the decision – both good and bad?

There are all sorts of issues to consider where you may know the background and be able to predict what is happening (particularly if you have carried out a PEST analysis) or where you would be advised to seek the opinion of someone not so caught up in the events as you are. However, as before, try to select someone whose opinion you really value and who will not come up with some of the clichés above! Perhaps a useful saying to remember is 'If you always do what you've always done, you'll always get what you've always got'. And if by the time you reach the end of this book you are genuinely happy with 'what you've always got', fine.

CASE STUDIES

Jane gains a new lease of life

Jane has progressed tremendously since attending her courses. There is a new air of enthusiasm in everything she does, and colleagues and friends have commented on this. She remains level-headed and cautious and knows that it would be easy to fall into an unrealistic mental state with her new-found enthusiasm. She has even considered whether she can maintain this new zest in her current role as a teacher, but she knows that, fundamentally, the work does not offer her the creativity and sense of being her own boss that she craves.

She has considered joining or establishing a co-operative venture for her craft work, knowing that in many cases these work extremely successfully. She has researched the topic carefully, but decides that the joint ownership of every aspect of the business does not appeal to her and that she needs independence. Fortunately for Jane, she knows that she can join the supply teacher list in her area and that this will be a most valuable financial support to her in the early stages. It will not be professionally rewarding, for she knows how supply teachers are often marginalised in schools, but the financial lifeline it offers is one which few other jobs can offer and she is immensely aware of her good fortune here. At the moment, Jane is in the fortunate position of having nothing to lose.

Francis recognises the limits

Buoyed up by the decisions he has already taken, Francis now realises that he needs a secure framework within which to operate. It is something which matters to him deeply and he knows that he lacks the self-discipline to go it alone in any venture. However, he also realises that he needs greater autonomy than he has had hitherto and that his previous working environment, which he had considered the norm, was in fact a straightjacket. There were certainly lost opportunities but he hadn't seen them and the culture of the bank had not encouraged any of his colleagues to seek them.

It's no use bewailing those now – the future is what Francis must focus on. Something with greater autonomy yet with an externally-imposed discipline – that's what he's seeking now.

Ramish is banking on a new future

Feeling a new lease of life from his recent activities, Ramish now also considers that he is prepared to take both a professional and a financial risk. He researches carefully all the aspects of establishing his own complementary medicine practice – additional market research about likely demand, possible funding sources, appropriate premises within the locality, set-up costs, additional qualifications/professional registrations he might seek in order to offer a wider range of services and the feasibility of bringing in other professionals.

He approaches his local bank for details of starting his own business and receives a helpful starter pack and video guide from them. He also consults the range of self-help books available to give him better background knowledge.

CHECKLIST SUMMARY

In this chapter we have considered:

- Your attitude to life in general.
- The aspects of working life you value.
- The importance of making decisions.

ACTION POINTS

- Clarify in your own mind the element of risk you are prepared to accept.
- Without making elaborate arrangements which nullify the benefit of any decision you make, list any back-up safety nets available.

8
Where Are You Going Next?

MAKING THE MOST OF CHOICES

As you have seen throughout this book, life is about making decisions. With every decision, clearly there are choices. There are choices about lifestyle – not merely the level of income you desire, but the means to achieve that. The style and the nature of the work you are involved with may be as important as the employment or business sector you select. Choices are not only about what you want to do but, just as importantly, what you *don't* want to do.

> **In aiming for a particular lifestyle you must balance risks against gains – potential benefits against potential drawbacks. You must balance the known, or at least the likely, against the unknown or the unlikely.**

By this stage of the book, and your own voyage of self-discovery, you will have a clearer idea about a number of issues:

- your motivations, your aspirations, your fears, your strengths and your weaknesses;
- the type of lifestyle you are seeking;
- whether you are aiming for full-time permanent employment, part-time employment, self-employment, a consultancy portfolio or, indeed, no employment of any type.

You will not be alone in your decision to change – The Office for National Statistics says that 16 per cent of the British workforce, or 3.3 million people, change jobs or work each year. However, unlike the majority of them, you will be different. Whatever decision you have made will have been based on what you have learnt about yourself; your assessment of the types of skills and knowledge you have to market;

your evaluation of the market-place in which you might operate and the working environment in which you feel you will grow personally and professionally. Consequently, you will not necessarily have to read through all the information below but just that which applies to your chosen destination.

ACCESSING SUPPORT NETWORKS

If you are already in employment, and you are aiming to remain within that employment sector, you will probably know of the support networks available in your line of work. For example, the Institute of Management provides members seeking to enhance their management skills and expertise not only a monthly magazine and a quarterly journal, but also an extensive list of publications under its own imprint, a library in their Corby headquarters which can be accessed by post and a wide range of courses at different levels which can be followed by open-learning or at a local centre, such as a further education college.

Seeking further employment in a sector in which you have already worked
You can try:

- professionally-linked support in your own sector
- professional bodies/societies
- trades unions
- web-sites.

Seeking a different line of employment in another sector
You can try:

- that sector's professional bodies
- professional publications in that sector.

Seeking self-employment or portfolio employment
You can try your local:

- Training & Enterprise Council (TEC)
- Tax Information Centre (TIC)
- Chamber of Commerce
- branch of the Federation of Small Businesses
- further education college.

Seeking further education or training in your specialism

Also if you wish to try something completely different, you can contact the organisations or view the websites listed in the Useful Addresses section on page 109.

MANAGING TIME

Managing time is a constant source of pressure for many people who feel that they have too many responsibilities for the time available. Some people are better time managers than others – they like to be organised, can prioritise, can project ahead and work backwards by allocating tasks to meet specific deadlines. There are many books published on time management (see Further Reading), but a useful way to prioritise tasks is to use the **MSC** approach.

At the start of any given day, make a written list of the tasks facing you – this is always good practice for your diary anyway. Think of all those tasks as an archer's target as shown in Figure 17.

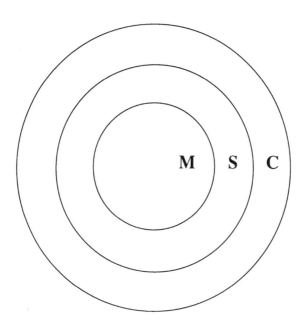

Fig. 17. The must, should and could do target.

Divide your tasks into three categories:

- Tasks which you **must** do (**M**). These are important, urgent and non-negotiable tasks. Failing to complete them will cause major inconvenience for yourself, colleagues, customers or suppliers. There is no way you can avoid these tasks.

- Tasks which you **should** do (**S**). These are less important and less urgent than those at the centre of the target. You can delay these until you have the M tasks completed. However, if you delay them too long, they will simply become 'must do' tasks. Plan ahead and aim to complete (or at least make a start) on these before they become urgent.

- Tasks which you **could** do (**C**). These are currently unimportant and time devoted to them will only detract from completing other more important tasks. Indeed, you might ask yourself 'What would be the consequence of not doing this task?' If there is no significant problem, why do it anyway?

Don't fool yourself that there is nothing which you can omit or which is less important than other tasks. If some tasks are more important, it follows that others are less important. In recognising this, you are prioritising and are on your way to managing your time.

MANAGING STRESS

An additional source of support or advice may be your home insurance company. Many companies now have a confidential helpline which you can access 24 hours a day for advice about stress management or healthcare. Check your policy for details.

Additionally, many trade unions and professional associations also provide such a service for their members. Again, check your membership pack for details.

Some employers also offer stress counselling or stress management courses. Check with your staff development office, if you have one. Some courses may be available anonymously or out of hours so that your line manager does not have to countersign your application form or agree to your attending. This can be advantageous because it may be the line manager who is causing some of the stress!

MARKETING YOURSELF

The term marketing does not just mean selling. Of course you will be selling yourself through your services, expertise or experience, perhaps to the highest bidder, but marketing is much more sophisticated than that. It involves:

- researching carefully your potential market/s
- establishing what your product/service portfolio is
- establishing a specific benefit (in quality, range, speed of service, flexibility, etc) which no competitor can offer – your *unique selling proposition*
- establishing a specific market where what you offer is of clear value and worth.

This would be equally true whether your market is as an employee targeting an employer or as a consultant marketing his/her services. Yet the highest bidder is not necessarily the most appropriate home for your services. Before you commit yourself to one purchaser, whether it be as an employee, a freelance or business, you would be wise to establish some rules of engagement. Depending on whether you are approaching someone as an employee, as a consultant or trader, you will wish to find out what the purchaser has on offer. These would include the following.

If considering employment

- Apart from income, what else can the employer offer you?
- What about professional or personal development?
- What about encouragement to pursue qualifications or gain additional experience?
- How much autonomy will you be allowed in the post?
- How much scope is there for independent thought or actions?
- Where can you aim for in the future?
- What if the company/organisation contracts: how will you continue to gain the employability skills you have been developing through this book?

If considering self-employment

Perhaps you have decided on self-employment or to start a business. As you develop your product or service portfolio, you may gain a deal with a particular customer.

- Is it a once-only deal?
- Is there the opportunity for repeat business?
- Is there scope for you to offer similar, related products or services so that the purchaser might buy a complete package?
- What facilities, services or opportunities can the purchaser provide for you which might make the work easier, more pleasant, more stimulating or reliable?
- What level of expenses will the purchaser provide, or are you expected to pick up the tab for all of these?
- On what basis will the purchaser be paying: weekly, monthly, after each delivery?
- What time lag is there between delivery and payment: instant, at the end of the month, after two months?

MAINTAINING YOUR EMPLOYABILITY

Having read this book, at the back of your mind should always be the question *'How do I maintain my employability?'* You will be only too familiar by now that having certain skills and knowledge at one moment in time does not mean that such skills will always be sought. Knowledge and skills can atrophy and die, and one must be constantly conscious of changing needs and demands, retaining flexibility and adaptability.

For example, at the time of writing many organisation are seeking computer experts who can make their computer system Year 2000-compliant in order to avoid the 'millenium bug'. At this stage, such consultants can command high fees, say £600 a day. This means that smaller companies cannot afford the fees unless their system inadequacies can be quickly and easily overcome. But what is the cost of *not* paying this? As the year 2000 gets closer, companies will find that they will need to pay more than this to avert crisis on 31 December 1999. After that date, there will be a short time when such consultants can probably charge the earth to remedy short-term problems. But after that, their skills will no longer be needed – it will be too late or organisations will simply have bought new, compliant systems. If the consultants have not kept up to date with other developments in the computing world, they will have no other skills to sell. You might argue that at that daily rate they will be able to take time off to learn new skills. Maybe, but that is no use to a company which, impressed with their work, wants at short notice to extend or develop their computer operations. It won't want to wait, won't be impressed with the delay and will find someone who can do the work.

> **Whatever the situation – as an employee or as a business – stay in touch with developments, predict the trends, gain the skills and knowledge and be able to market your flexibility and adaptability where others get left behind.**

APPLYING FOR JOBS

Assuming that you wish to gain an employed post with an organisation, the most common way of achieving that still remains the job application. This process is divided into a number of stages which are given in the flowchart in Figure 18. This sequence holds true for most organisations although there may be some differences about, for example, whether candidates are interviewed on the same day or over a period of time and when references are taken up. Some organisations do this after the interview so that they are not swayed in interview by someone else's opinion.

In order to reach the interview it is likely that you will be asked to complete some or all of the following.

Completing the application form

Apart from very small organisations, most concerns have a **job application form** which allows them to ask the same questions in the same sequence to all candidates. Clearly this has advantages in terms of fairness and consistency, but not all application forms are well designed, with the needs of the applicant accounted for. Some forms may be very cramped, have lots of space allocated for internal personnel department use, be repetitive or not allow the candidates to expand on key areas such as past experience.

Tips for completing an application form

- Match up your experience to the qualities and experience sought.
- Follow instructions such as 'use black ink' or 'use block capitals'.
- Don't leave gaps.
- Practise on a photocopy to maximise spacing and layout.
- Keep a copy for future reference.

It is becoming increasingly common with some large organisations to use a computer to scan through applications for **key words**. If the job advertisement has demanded 'experience of using Access databases',

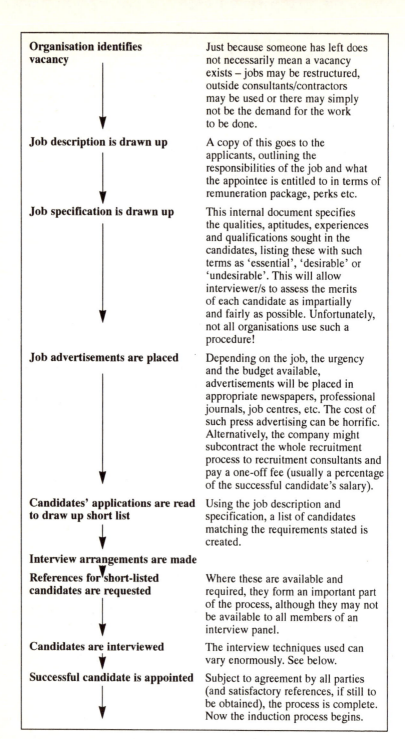

Organisation identifies vacancy	Just because someone has left does not necessarily mean a vacancy exists – jobs may be restructured, outside consultants/contractors may be used or there may simply not be the demand for the work to be done.
Job description is drawn up	A copy of this goes to the applicants, outlining the responsibilities of the job and what the appointee is entitled to in terms of remuneration package, perks etc.
Job specification is drawn up	This internal document specifies the qualities, aptitudes, experiences and qualifications sought in the candidates, listing these with such terms as 'essential', 'desirable' or 'undesirable'. This will allow interviewer/s to assess the merits of each candidate as impartially and fairly as possible. Unfortunately, not all organisations use such a procedure!
Job advertisements are placed	Depending on the job, the urgency and the budget available, advertisements will be placed in appropriate newspapers, professional journals, job centres, etc. The cost of such press advertising can be horrific. Alternatively, the company might subcontract the whole recruitment process to recruitment consultants and pay a one-off fee (usually a percentage of the successful candidate's salary).
Candidates' applications are read to draw up short list	Using the job description and specification, a list of candidates matching the requirements stated is created.
Interview arrangements are made	
References for short-listed candidates are requested	Where these are available and required, they form an important part of the process, although they may not be available to all members of an interview panel.
Candidates are interviewed	The interview techniques used can vary enormously. See below.
Successful candidate is appointed	Subject to agreement by all parties (and satisfactory references, if still to be obtained), the process is complete. Now the induction process begins.

Fig. 18 Job application flowchart.

'able to demonstrate initiative', 'educated to A level/NVQ Level 3 standard' or 'minimum of five years' experience in fast-moving consumer goods', the scanning process will pick up these terms and reject any other applications, no matter how good they may be otherwise. So always ensure that you use the key terms demanded.

Devising your curriculum vitae

A **curriculum vitae** is usually demanded for most jobs, and certainly for those where there is no application form. The CV sets out in a structured manner your past relevant history. There are many books on devising a CV and this is not the place to go into detail. However, here are some tips for compiling a CV.

- A CV must always be typed/word processed.

- Devise different CVs for different types of employment so that you can stress different skills and experiences.

- Present your employment history in reverse chronological order (unless you have very limited employment history).

- Ensure that your CV looks attractively set out but avoid coloured paper, pretty bows or any other distractions.

- Limit the length of your CV to two single-sided sheets of A4 paper.

- Use the CV to emphasise experiences/qualities which it may be difficult to explain in an application form.

Writing your letter of application

Some organisations request a **letter of application**. It is always beneficial to include one, even as a covering letter. The letter offers you the opportunity to expand upon and to emphasise points which you may be able to refer to only briefly in your CV or application form. It allows you to sell yourself as a personality. A good letter can be a very powerful weapon in your favour. A poor letter will consign your application to the bin.

Tips for writing a letter of application

- Take note of whether the instructions say the letter should be typed or handwritten – if you have a choice, make that decision based on the quality of your handwriting.

- Present yourself in a positive and confident light.

- Don't refer to your current or previous employer in a negative way.

- Take care with spelling, punctuation and phrasing.

- Use the appropriate ending depending on whether you know the name of the individual you are writing to. If a given name, end *Yours sincerely,* if a title *Yours faithfully.*

PREPARING FOR YOUR INTERVIEW

The principal aim of a good application, of course, is to gain an interview. When you are called to interview, you should treat this invitation accordingly – it shows that you have impressed on paper and the employer wants to learn more about you.

Before the interview

- Re-read your application.
- Carry out some further research on the organisation and the job.
- Consider the types of question you might be asked – both general and job-specific.
- Consider your strengths for the post.
- Consider your wider strengths as an employee of the organisation.
- Identify some 'allowable' weakness.
- Be positive about your chances.
- Arrive on time.
- Dress appropriately.

During the interview

- Make eye contact with all the interviewers.
- Answer questions directly – don't waffle.
- Have a question ready to show that you have prepared and are taking an interest in the organisation.
- If you are interviewed on the same day as other candidates, keep your own counsel when you are alone with them – don't give away your own strengths.

- Smile but don't grin.
- Keep your body language positive.

As with the section on job applications, take the opportunity to consult a book dealing with this topic. See Further Reading for details.

CASE STUDIES

Jane prepares to take the plunge

With the end of the summer term in sight, Jane has steadily been building up her client base and her order book. She has plenty to keep her occupied during the six-week holiday period, but also makes a particular effort to seek information from the head so that she can build in planning for next term's work. Jane still has sufficient professionalism to ensure that her pupils and colleagues do not suffer because she is making alternative career arrangements.

Jane speaks with her pension provider and makes arrangements to buy in additional years and also researches the personal pensions market for when she becomes self-employed. She budgets for this in her plans and knows that it would be short-sighted to overlook this commitment. Being a believer in 'personal privatisation', she does not wish to end up in the 'misery gap' when she finally finishes work.

Jane now feels ready to take the plunge in a year's time. She has started to draw up an action plan so that she can ensure that various strategies and arrangements are in place for when she leaves. She realises that her timetabling experience in school has been helpful in creating this schedule.

Francis makes progress

Francis makes some tentative enquiries about similar employment in the same sector or in self-employment. The latter he rules out, feeling that he lacks the necessary qualities to make a success of this. There are some possibilities with other employers, but he rapidly learns that the working environment is similar in all financial institutions.

He makes a few applications for several internal posts at the regional head office and gets further than ever before in his applications. The prospect of a job at regional level appeals now as he is realising those latent skills and strengths within. He is optimistic and enjoying life more than he has for a long time.

Ramish continues on his path

Ramish is making progress with his enquiries about setting up a private practice. He is currently seeking advice from his professional body, who are supportive. In his own time he is attending a brief marketing course at his local college and is drawing up a business plan. Things are going well and he is particularly pleased by the interest and support of his colleagues. Even one of the senior managers has dropped in to chat with him, expressing his admiration for the courageous way Ramish wants to implement his plans.

CHECKLIST SUMMARY

In this chapter we have considered:

- The importance of making choices.
- Some sources of support.
- The job application and interview process.
- Good practice for job applications and interviews.

ACTION POINTS

- How much development has there been with the opportunities you foresaw for yourself at the end of the last chapter?
- If this is too early, what deadline are you setting yourself to see some development?

9
Action Planning

DEVISING AN ACTION PLAN

By this stage you should feel reasonably confident about what you have discovered about yourself, your motivations, your aspirations and where you are most likely to find fulfilling and rewarding work. However, it is very easy to let your enthusiasm and good intentions drift. So you need a structure to help you keep focused and to check whether you are achieving your objectives. This is where an **action plan** comes in.

An action plan is simply a plan of action – it's no more difficult than that – but, for it to work effectively, a useful mnemonic to remember is **SMART**. An action plan should be:

- **S**pecific
- **M**easurable
- **A**chievable
- **R**ealistic
- **T**ime-bound.

1. Your short-term aims
Aims for the next six months:

Things I want to change in the workplace

- S..
- M..
- A..
- R..
- T..

Things I want to change about my life-style

- S..
- M..

- A. . . . .
- R. . . . .
- T. . . . .

Things I want to change about me

- S. . . . .
- M . . . .
- A. . . . .
- R. . . . .
- T . . . .

My sources of support

- Financial: . . . .
- People: . . . .

How will I know if I have achieved my aims?
. . . .

2. Your medium-term aims
Aims for six months to two years:

Things I want to change in the workplace

- S. . . . .
- M . . . .
- A. . . . .
- R. . . . .
- T . . . .

Things I want to change about my life-style

- S. . . . .
- M . . . .
- A. . . . .
- R. . . . .
- T . . . .

Things I want to change about me

- S. . . . .
- M . . . .

- A. . . . .
- R. . . . .
- T. . . . .

My sources of support

- Financial: . . . .
- People: . . . .

How will I know if I have achieved my aims?
. . . .

3. Your long-term aims
Aims for two years or longer:

Where I want to be

- S. . . . .
- M . . . .
- A. . . . .
- R. . . . .
- T. . . . .

What I want to be doing
. . . .

How I want life to be
. . . .

How will I know if I have achieved my aims?
. . . .

KEEPING YOURSELF IN MIND

You should be at the forefront of your thoughts in your planning. This is not selfishness – you have already identified those others who are dear to you and for whom you have responsibilities. You are already taking their needs into account in your planning. Furthermore, by being pro-active, you are taking much more control of the situation than just waiting for things to happen to you (and to them), over which you have no control.

However, it is easy to get dissuaded from your plans and to let time catch up. To help overcome this you will find it beneficial to keep a clear note of:

- your intentions
- your plans
- your targets.

PRIORITISING ACTIVITIES

If you want to make the most out of life, you will be seeking new opportunities and challenges. Sometimes there may be too many to choose from and so you will have to consider which of these you should pick. You may need to remind yourself of your core purpose, of what you really want to achieve.

For example if Jane, still remaining as a primary school teacher, were to join one of the school working parties, which of the following might be of the greatest help to her in her plans (assuming that her contributions were of equal value to the school)?

- marketing
- assessment
- boys' sports
- school uniform.

Marketing would clearly seem to be the obvious choice – it could teach Jane a great deal about the fundamentals of marketing her own wares also, albeit in a different context. She would certainly gain far more than from the others whose values and aims would not be congruent with her own. With those, she could well discover that she was putting in a lot of additional effort to gain little knowledge and few skills which were transferable to her own situation. Yet, by volunteering for the marketing working party, Jane would not only be able to gain directly and relevantly herself, but also to contribute her growing expertise and maintain goodwill. As indicated earlier, employability skills cut both ways and will never be lost on your current employer.

TALKING YOURSELF UP

Making decisions to change fundamental aspects of your life or to retain the same position but with a different perspective on life can be hard. The value of having someone with whom you can talk openly has already been stressed. Vital also is the quality of feedback which you get from others. But you also need feedback from yourself, to motivate you by recognising what you have achieved and how you can meet your targets. The following tips can help:

- Identify your continuing achievements.
- Quantify the progress you have made.
- Reflect on what you have done and ask yourself: 'In order to carry out that task, what skills and abilities do I have? What do I need to be good at to do this?'
- List your skills and abilities!

Take the time to talk yourself. This could be whilst sitting at traffic lights, on the train home or as you go to sleep. You can do so silently if necessary! Say 'Well done', give yourself a metaphorical pat on the back and take pride in what you have done. In other words, as the saying goes, 'Make an appointment with yourself'.

EVALUATING PROGRESS

Such motivational small-talk may not always be easy and you should not get carried away with false praise. It should be balanced with constructive criticism of where you feel you still need to improve, such as in the example below:

> 'That meeting was pretty awful, wasn't it? I rushed through my point of view, didn't do my homework on how Jones would react, and didn't have a clear answer to the problem with deadlines. How stupid! Still, I know how to handle that in future: check out the likely impact on Jones' department, take my time with the proposals (maybe prepare some overhead transparencies) and check all my facts in advance.'

Things will not always go well and you need to have the courage to evaluate your own progress and to improve any shortcomings in your own expectations of yourself.

EVALUATING BY CONSIDERING KEY POINTS

- Keep your targets in mind and review them regularly.
- Praise your achievements.
- Evaluate where and why some things have not gone so well.
- Identify the causes of this.
- Try to remedy the situation by setting achievable targets.
- If necessary, be realistic and revise your targets or time-scales.

CASE STUDIES

Jane
Having set herself a target of a year's time before leaving, Jane estab-

lishes some key targets and deadlines as part of her action plan. She is now six months into this and everything seems to be going well. She knows that initially things will be tough and that she will need extra financial support. She approaches a supply teaching agency and enrols on their books. She knows that the pay will be less than she currently gets, that it can be hard going into a new school at very short notice and that supply teachers often get a raw deal. Nevertheless, it's a tremendous lifeline to her. However, she also knows that she must not become complacent about this and that if her new career is really going to work she has to be self-supporting as quickly as possible. She has given herself two years in her long-term action plan to do this.

Francis

Francis hears good news about his application for a post in the regional office. After a series of interviews, he is appointed to a post which has an emphasis on systems and structures. It will be his responsibility to explain these and implement them with colleagues. Francis feels that he is well suited to this post – it encompasses some of the aspects about which he feels strongly but is also going to make use of his new-found skills in explaining complexities in simple language. It is a real challenge to Francis but one he relishes and feels ready for as a 'techno-realist'.

Francis has decided to stay with the same employer. He has done so after considerable soul-searching and research into alternatives. But he stays, having learnt a great deal more about himself and the organisation and with a much greater sense of self-confidence. Some of his personal values have changed, he has become more honest with himself and, whilst he looks forward to his new post with enthusiasm, he also feels more confident about his own future employability skills. He knows that he must keep his own personal agenda to the fore and not slip back into becoming merely a company man.

Ramish

Ramish decides to take up the opportunity to go into practice with a private-practice osteopath who is planning to retire in the next two years. The health trust agrees to his request to keep him on the books for the next six months in a part-time capacity to cover a colleague's maternity leave. He also negotiates a contract to buy in his services privately in order to reduce waiting lists. This will be at a lower rate than he could charge patients directly but it is an assured income and gives some welcome stability over the next two years.

Ramish's principal concern, and where he devotes much of his planning, is in building up a practice which can offer a variety of complementary medical services. The premises are right and the owner sees it as a way of reducing his overheads, limiting his personal involvement to that of a 'sleeping partner'. This will make the practice more saleable, particularly as Ramish will be putting in his own time and expertise. Ramish takes clear legal and financial advice on this so that it works in his favour. Ramish is delighted with the way things are working out – he feels a sense of control over his destiny once more and that he is able to live out his values again.

CHECKLIST SUMMARY

In this final chapter we have considered:

- The importance of devising action plans.
- The importance of evaluating and reviewing action plans.
- The importance of keeping motivated.
- And finally, the importance of you.

These are your action points for your future.

POSTSCRIPT

At times things will be difficult, you may feel alone, you may feel that your 'sad captains' have deserted you, and that you alone are responsible for the decisions you make. But ultimately, you will have the satisfaction of knowing that you have taken more control of your life, and that, whatever decisions you make, they are ones with which you can live. This feeling is eloquently expressed in the poem *The Road Not Taken* by the American poet Robert Frost:

Two roads diverged in a wood, and I –
I took the one less travelled by,
and that has made all the difference.

You too, like Jane and Ramish, may reject the well-worn path, the apparently clearly laid out route, the route taken by the crowd. Or, like Francis, you may decide that as you have already started on this path and you are committed to it, as you have tended and nurtured it, it is too late to turn back or to take a side-track. For you the benefits of the well-worn path outweigh the risks of losing your way, of unknown obstacles and a lack of clear sign-posting on the less-travelled path.

Whichever decision you make, you know that it is based on what you now understand about yourself and where you want to go. Whichever road you take – well-worn or less travelled by – enjoy it.

Glossary

Accreditation of Prior Learning (APL). Giving credit for previous learning and achievement which may have taken place. It is common in **NVQ** qualifications to enhance flexibility of learning and to save going over ground with which learner is familiar and in which s/he is competent. Sometimes known as:

Accreditation of Prior Experience and Learning (APEL). Similar to above but relevant experience is also credited. A bona fide concept when rigorously implemented but beware 'offshore' universities which will credit 'students' with degrees in return for a steep fee and mere claims of previous experience.

Contingency worker. Employment or jobs being reliant upon demand. If demand dips and there are no other tasks for the worker, his/her employment ceases.

Curriculum vitae. Commonly abbreviated to CV, this literally means 'an outline of your life'. Frequently used as a standard means of listing previous experience and qualifications when applying for work.

Distance learning (DL). Where learning takes place physically away from the education provider (eg correspondence courses, learning via the Internet and some aspects of the Open University's provision). See also **flexible learning** and **open learning**.

Downshift. To take lower status work, including perhaps self-employment, because the perceived benefits (eg autonomy and variety) outweigh the perceived losses (eg perceived status, company infrastructure, etc).

EDAP (employee development assistance programme). A facility whereby employees are allocated and encouraged to use a 'voucher' entitling them to education at the employer's expense. Ford and Rover have well known schemes.

Eleven-plus. The examination formerly sat by most pupils in Britain at age 11 in order to determine whether they attended a grammar school (20 per cent) or a secondary-modern school (80 per cent). Abolished in most areas with the introduction of all-ability, comprehensive schools.

Employability. Retaining your attractiveness to employers through updating the skills, qualities and attributes you can offer.

Flexible learning. The use of learning packages which can be used flexibly, eg within or away from a learning establishment, as a means of delivering a complete course or just part of it. See also **distance learning** and **open learning**.

Global economy. Using the full potential of achieving economies of scale through sourcing materials, utilising cheap labour and maximising market penetration on a world-wide scale.

Job. A social contract into which we enter with an employer to spend an agreed number of hours per week in his/her employment in exchange for a certain sum of money which allows us, within financial constraints, to spend in the way we wish to pursue a particular lifestyle.

Job-share. Division of the roles and tasks in a single job between two people (usually equally) who also share the income and benefits associated with that job. This facility promotes flexibility and can ensure that people who have other commitments (eg single parents or part-time students) can also access the labour market.

Learning Age. The name of the Government Green Paper (February 1998) which emphasised the importance of developing skills and knowledge for both employability and personal fulfilment in the next century.

Learning credits. A system to encourage ownership of learning whereby all learning and training is entered on a smart-card, thereby encouraging the learner to take advantage of opportunities offered to build up a bank of recognised knowledge, skills and qualifications.

Listening noises. Noises which give feedback to the speaker/s to show that you are listening, eg 'Yes, I see', 'OK, right' etc.

Life-mapping. Charting the most significant events in one's life in order to understand the consequences of these events and their impact upon the individual.

Mind-set. Mental attitude and set of values. Those with a mind-set which does not expect an employer to offer or provide a lifelong job, or who actively seek alternative means of employment, will develop greater employability skills than those who have a passive expectation that the employer will provide for ever.

Misery gap. The difference between actual pension income and that needed to achieve a comfortable retirement.

Motivation theories. Theories on the way in which people are encouraged through positive motivation or coerced, threatened and bullied through negative motivation to improve their performance. The examples dealt with suggest that individuals respond differently according to their needs and personality.

National Curriculum. The range and level of subjects which children in British state schools study between the ages of 5 and 16.

National Health Service (NHS). The provision of state-funded medical and dental care in the UK.

Open learning (OL): Although there is no universally agreed definition of OL, the essential concept is of opening up new opportunities to learn. This can be done by, for example, enabling learners to study whatever, wherever and whenever they like and at a pace which suits them. See also **flexible learning** and **distance learning**.

Paramedic. Someone engaged in a supporting medical role, eg, Ramish in this book is an osteopath, supporting the work of orthopaedic surgeons, GPs and physiotherapists. The latter also being a paramedic discipline.

Personal privatisation. Increased personal responsibility for the costs of pensions provision, welfare, educational and health costs.

PEST analysis. Analysis of political, economic, social trends and technological changes which may affect a business. Used here to consider impact of such changes on the individual's employability.

Portfolio. A varied collection of work and responsibilities with a variety of clients or employers.

Production line. Organisation of production in a factory according to set procedures, sequences and costings. It has been traditional to employ people to carry out a single task only in the production.

Psychometric testing. A series of written/graphical or other tests to determine an individual's psychological profile. Employers use such tests to screen out applicants before final selection. Alternatively, a number of psychological counselling services use such tests to advice individuals which careers/job sectors/types of employment they seem most suited/unsuited to (check in broadsheet newspapers for addresses – mostly London – of such services).

Purchaser/provider. Current National Health Service split whereby the Area Health Authorities (the purchasers) decide which medical, clinical, nursing and paramedic services to buy from hospital trusts, GP surgeries, dental practices, chiropodists, etc. The latter are the providers of medical care.

Resiliency. Having the strength of character to take the knocks and setbacks inevitable in today's working environment.

Self-actualisation. Achieving one's full potential. Maslow's concept is based on the premise in Robert Browning's poem, Andrea del Sarto:

'Ah, but a Man's reach should exceed his grasp, Or what's a heaven for?'

SME. A small or medium-sized enterprise. By definition, this is one employing between 50 and 300 people. In many areas of the UK (eg Wales), the greatest economic growth is in SMEs. For many people this marks a shift in culture because they may have previously worked only for large organisations. For graduates in particular, the prospect of working for an SME rather than for traditional corporate graduate-employers has to be contemplated.

SWOT analysis. An analysis of one's strengths, weaknesses, opportunities and threats. Frequently conducted by businesses in order to establish how they should develop, but can be applied to an individual's circumstances also.

Techno-realist. Someone with a realistic attitude to the opportunities, demands and implications of new (ie computer-related) technology. His/her views contrasts with those of a **technophile** (who is obsessed with the technology and can see no dangers in it) and a **techno-luddite** (who resents anything to do with new technology).

Transferable skills. Those skills which can be used in a variety of contexts whether in the workplace or in leisure, eg communication skills, keyboard skills, time-management skills.

Vendor-mindedness. Being aware of how to sell your services, skills, knowledge, experience and attributes to a purchaser in return for a fee.

Useful Addresses

INFORMATION OF FINANCING FURTHER/HIGHER EDUCATION OPPORTUNITIES

Career Development Loans, Freepost, Newcastle-upon-Tyne NE85 1BR. Tel: (0800) 585505. Offers loans from £300 to £8,000 to be paid back at preferential rates only when training or education is completed. Arranged through certain high street banks but all information co-ordinated by DfEE at above address.

The Student Loans Company Ltd, 100 Bothwell Street, Glasgow G2 7JD. Tel: (0800) 405010. Website: http://www.slc.co.uk. Administers loans on behalf of DfEE for accredited courses in higher education.

Student Awards Agency for Scotland, Gyleview House, 3 Redheughs Rigg, South Gyle, Edinburgh EH12 9HH. Tel: (0131) 244 5823. Currently student awards in Scotland are co-ordinated through this agency, whereas in England and Wales it is through the student's local council.

Financial Times Management, Portland Tower, Portland Street M1 3LD. Tel: (0161) 245 3300. Fax: (0161) 245 3301. Co-ordinates a wide range of 'open learning' courses offered via further education colleges or direct.

Open College of the Arts, Houndshill, Warsbrough, Barnsley, South Yorks S70 6TU. Tel: (01226) 730495. Fax: (01226) 730838. Email: open.arts@ukonline.co.uk. Website: www.web.ukonline.co.uk/open.arts/index/htm.

INFORMATION OR ADVICE ON FURTHER TRAINING OR EDUCATION

DfEE (Department for Education & Employment), Publications Centre, PO Box 2193, London E15 2EU. Tel: (0181) 533 2000.

DfEE Lifelong Learning website: www.lifelonglearning.co.uk. Provides a range of information on opportunities in lifelong learning across the UK and also information on Career Development Loans.

ECCTIS, the government-supported computerised course information service. Gives comprehensive information on 100,000 courses throughout the UK. Available through educational institutions, adult guidance centres, some libraries.

Move on up! Website:http//www.lloydsbank.co.uk/moveonup. Designed by this author primarily for school/college leavers, the website nevertheless gives general information about applying for higher education.

National Council for Vocational Qualifications (NCVQ), 222 Euston Road, London NW1 2BZ. Tel: (0171) 728 1893.

Universities & Colleges Admissions Service (UCAS), Fulton House, Jessop Avenue, Cheltenham, Glos GL50 3SH. Tel: (01242) 222444. Fax: (01242) 221622. Website: http://www.ucas.ac.uk

HIGHER EDUCATION PROVIDERS SPECIALISING IN ADULT LEARNERS

Extra-Mural Departments/Departments of Adult Continuing Education. See your local press and telephone directory (under Universities) for details. Most universities have community education programmes.

Birkbeck College, University of London. Offers over 100 degree evening programmes and over 1,000 short courses, certificates and diplomas throughout London area. Website: http//www.bbk.ac.uk. Email: admissions@admin.bbk.ac.uk. Prospectus line: Degrees and Master's courses: 0845 601 0174 (lo-call number), short courses, certificates and diplomas: Tel: (0171) 631 6687.

Open University, General Enquiry Service, PO Box 200, Milton Keynes MK7 6YZ. Tel: (01908) 274066. Open University telephone hotline (24 hrs): (0870) 900 0304. Website: http://www.open.ac.uk/ou/study.html. Globally-renowned for high quality materials and courses.

RESIDENTIAL HIGHER EDUCATION FOR ADULTS

Coleg Harlech, Harlech, Gwynedd LL46 2PU. Tel: 01766 780363. Website: http://www.harlech.ac.uk. Offers HE Diplomas and is tailored to providing courses for mature students without traditional entry qualifications.

Ruskin College, Walton Street, Oxford OX1 2HE. Tel: (01865) 554331. Well-established institution with strong trade-union links, with long heritage of providing for those not traditionally able to access educational opportunities.

DISTANCE-LEARNING CENTRES OFFERING MBAs etc

See newspapers advertisements, particularly in *Guardian* (Tuesday), *Daily Telegraph* (Wednesday).

OPEN AND DISTANCE-LEARNING WEBSITES

Open University (OU) Online courses. Presents information on and descriptions of courses available; computer hardware and software requirements to take Internet courses. Email: Internet-Course-Enquiries@open.ac.uk. Website: http://cszx.open.ac.uk/zx.

The Online Netskills Interactive Course (TONIC). Outlines course based at University of Newcastle offering information and practical guidance on Internet topics. Email: netskills-admin@netskills.ac.uk. Website: http://www.netskills.ac.uk/TONIC.

IT COURSES

European Computer Driving Licence (ECDL). A recently-introduced qualification in the UK which has gained great success in Europe, particularly in Scandinavia where it has become a routinely sought qualification by employers. Available at a variety of locations across the UK, mostly FE colleges. For information contact: Pete Bayley, ECDL UK, The British Computer Society, 1 Sanford Street, Swindon, Wiltshire SN1 1HJ. Tel: (01793) 417494. Email: ecdl@hq.bcs.org.uk. Website: http://www.bcs.org.uk/ecdl/logbook.htm.

MANAGEMENT SUPPORT AND TRAINING

The Institute of Management, Management House, Cottingham Road, Corby, Northants NN17 1TT. Tel: (01536) 204222. Fax: (01536) 201651. Email: member@inst-mgt.org.uk. Website: http://www.inst-mgt.org.uk. For management resources guide on the web: http://inst-mgt.org.uk/external/mgt-link.html.

OPPORTUNITIES TO OFFER SKILLS TO OTHERS AND 'FIND ONESELF'

Camp America, 37a Queen's Gate, London SW7 5HR. Email: brochure@campamerica.co.uk. Website: http://www..aifs.org/iaifs-cam.htm. Offers suitable candidates up to nine weeks' summer experience as a youth leader in USA supervising children in camps, sports training etc. Free transatlantic flight, accommodation and meals.

Voluntary Services Overseas (VSO), 317 Putney Bridge Road, London SW15 2PN. Tel (0181) 780 7500. Website: http://www.oneworld. org/vso/. Offers suitable (graduate) candidates with specific skills placements in third world/emerging countries. Particularly needs candidates with teaching, engineering and agricultural expertise and qualifications.

JOB/RECRUITMENT LEADS

Your local Jobcentre (See telephone directory).

Your local newspaper/s. Check which day/evening features most entries for job vacancies.

National newspapers, especially if you are geographically mobile. Of particular benefit may be *The Daily Telegraph, The Daily Mail, The Daily Express* or *The Guardian*. Note also that the *Telegraph* has an Appointments Plus website (www.telegraph.co.uk) giving links to industry associations and to psychometric testing.

GROUP AND INDIVIDUAL SUPPORT IN EMPLOYABILITY SKILLS

Ashley Associates, 44 Gwerneinon Road, Derwen Fawr, Swansea SA2 8EW. Tel: (01792) 296223 Fax: (01792) 207702. Run by the author of this book. Offers courses in employability skills, job application and interview technique. Email: rodashley@btinternet.com

Self Renewal Group. Tel: (0171) 258 3951. Email: mitch@srg.co.uk. Website: http://www.srg.co.uk. Website pages useful for self-reflection.

TELEWORKING

TCA (The Telework, telecottage and Telecentre Association). This is Europe's largest organisation dedicated to the promotion of teleworking. Associated also with TCW (telecottages Wales), STA (Scottish Teleworking Association) and TWI (Telework Ireland). Membership helpline: (0800) 616008. Fax: (01453) 836174. Email: tca@venus.co.uk.

Further Reading

The following publications deal in more detail with many of the topics raised in this book.

Career Dynamics: Matching Individual and Organisational Needs, Edgar Schein (Addison-Wesley, 1978).
Guide to the Management Gurus, Carol Kennedy (Century Business, 1991).
How To Market Yourself, Ian Phillipson (How To Books, 1995).
Improve Your People Skills, Peter Honey (Institute of Personnel Management, 1988).
Interviews – How to succeed, Roderic Ashley (Tynron, 1990).
Jobshift, William Bridges (Nicholas Brealey, 1995).
Management Teams – Why they succeed or fail, R Meredith Belbin (Heinemann, 1982).
Motivation and Personality, Abraham Maslow (Harper & Row, 1970).
The Human Problems of an Industrial Civilisation, Elton Mayo (Macmillan, 1933).
The Human Side of Enterprise, Douglas McGregor (McGraw-Hill, 1960).
The Learning Age, HM Government Green Paper (HMSO, February 1998).
The Motivation to Work, Herzberg F, Mausner B, Snyderman B (Wiley, 1959).
The New Unblocked Manager, Dave Francis & Mike Woodcock (Gower, 1996).
The Seven Habits of Highly Effective People, Stephen R Covey (Simon & Schuster, 1989).
Transferable Personal Skills (2nd ed), David Hind & Rod Ashley (Business Education Publishers, 1994).
2020 Vision, The Henley Centre (Barclays Life, 1998).
Understanding Organisations, Charles Handy (Penguin, 1993).
When Giants Learn to Dance, Rosabeth Moss Kanter (Routledge, 1994).
Writing a CV That Works, Paul McGee (How To Books, 1997).

References

PREFACE

Acknowledgement: *Jobshift, How to prosper in a workplace without jobs*, William Bridges (Nicholas Brealey Publishing Ltd. Tel: (0171) 430 0224. Fax: (0171) 404 8311).

CHAPTER 1

1. *The Learning Age*, Introduction, Section 1.4, Government Green Paper (HMSO, February 1998).
2. *Ibid*, Chapter 2, 2.5.
3. The Henley Centre for Forecasting, 1998.
4. William Bridges, op. cit.

CHAPTER 6

1. The Henley Centre for Forecasting, June 1998.

Index

FINDING A JOB WITH A FUTURE
How to identify and work in growth industries and services

Laurel Alexander

If you want to ensure a long lasting career move in the right direction, you need to read this book which sets out in a practical way, growth areas of industry and commerce. Discover the work cycle of the future based on job specific skills, abstract skills, continuous learning and lifetime career planning. Learn about flexible ways of working. Laurel Alexander is a manager/trainer in career development who has helped many individuals succeed in changing their work direction.

144pp illus. 1 85703 310 8.

PASSING THAT INTERVIEW
Your step-by-step guide to coming out on top

Judith Johnstone

Using a systematic and practical approach, this book takes you step-by-step through the essential pre-interview groundwork, the interview encounter itself, and what you can learn from the experience. The book contains sample pre- and post-interview correspondence, and is complete with a guide to further reading, glossary of terms, and index. 'This is from the first class How To Books stable.' *Escape Committee Newsletter*. 'Offers a fresh approach to a well documented subject.' *Newscheck* (Careers Service Bulletin). 'A complete step-by-step guide.' *The Association of Business Executives*. Judith Johnstone is a Member of the Institute of Personnel & Development; she has been an instructor in Business Studies and adult literacy tutor, and has long experience of helping people at work.

144pp illus. 1 85703 538 0. 5th edition.

GETTING THAT JOB
The complete job finders handbook

Joan Fletcher

Now in its fourth edition this popular book provides a clear step-by-step guide to identifying job opportunities, writing successful application letters, preparing for interviews and being selected. 'A valuable book.' *Teachers Weekly*. 'Cheerful and appropriate . . . particularly helpful in providing checklists designed to bring system to searching for a job. This relaxed, friendly and very helpful little book could bring lasting benefit.' *Times Educational Supplement*. 'Clear and concise . . . should be mandatory reading by all trainees.' *Comlon Magazine* (LCCI). Joan Fletcher is an experienced Manager and Student Counsellor.

112pp illus. 1 85703 380 9. 4th edition.

STAYING AHEAD AT WORK
How to develop a winning portfolio of work skills and attitudes

Karen Mannering

The world of work is changing and employers are demanding more than just qualifications. To stay employed it is vital that you build a flexible portfolio of skills that say more about how you work and interact with others, than just the job you do. Getting ahead is tough, staying ahead can be tougher still. This book includes techniques to help you develop that 'something special' that will give you the edge over colleagues. You will also learn how to develop transportable soft skills that will ensure your future employability. Karen Mannering has worked extensively in the field of personal development, helping people build up a portfolio of skills that will enhance their professional careers.

128pp illus. 1 85703 298 5.

LEARNING NEW JOB SKILLS
How and where to obtain the right training to help you get on at work

Laurel Alexander

This book presents a positive approach to education and training and will enable you to make considered and informed choices about improving your job prospects. Taking a training course will improve your confidence, prepare you for a job with a future, potentially increase your earnings and bring fresh challenge back into your life. There are guidelines on how to get funding for training courses, getting vocational training if you are unemployed and returning to study as a mature student. Laurel Alexander is a specialist trainer and writer in career development and has helped hundreds of adults improve their working lives.

128pp illus. 1 85703 375 2.

WRITING A CV THAT WORKS
Developing and using your key marketing tool

Paul McGee

What makes a CV stand out from the crowd? How can you present yourself in the most successful way? This practical book shows you how to develop different versions of your CV for every situation. Reveal your hidden skills, identify your achievements and learn how to communicate these successfully. Different styles and uses for a CV are examined, as you discover the true importance of your most powerful marketing tool. Paul McGee is a freelance Trainer and Consultant for one of Britain's largest outplacement organisations. He conducts marketing workshops for people from all walks of life.

128pp illus. 1 85703 365 5. 2nd edition.

WRITING BUSINESS LETTERS
How to produce day-to-day correspondence that is clear and effective

Ann Dobson

Intended for absolute beginners, this book uses fictional characters in a typical business setting to contrast the right and wrong ways to go about things. Taking nothing for granted, the book shows: how to plan a letter, how to write and present it, how to deal with requests, how to write and answer complaints, standard letters, personal letters, job applications, letters overseas, and a variety of routine and tricky letters. Good, bad and middling examples are used to help beginners see for themselves the right and wrong ways of doing things. Ann Dobson is Principal of a secretarial training school with long experience of helping people strengthen their business skills.

183pp illus. 1 85703 491 0. 3rd edition.

STARTING TO MANAGE
How to prepare yourself for a more responsible role at work

Julie-Ann Amos

This practical book gives a broad overview of management, to dispel much of the mystery which surrounds it. It is intended for all new managers, supervisors, students and anyone who hopes to enter management. It explains the various basic theories and puts these into a practical everyday context. The reader will learn how to manage: workloads, decisions, stock, equipment, money, legislation, customers, staff, and much more besides.

160pp illus. 1 85703 319 1.